# DEVELOPMENT OF INSURANCE IN ANGOLA

Case Study of a Key African Frontier Insurance Market

ISRAEL MUCHENA

authorHOUSE®

AuthorHouse™ UK
1663 Liberty Drive
Bloomington, IN 47403  USA
www.authorhouse.co.uk
Phone: 0800.197.4150

Published by AuthorHouse  04/10/2019

ISBN: 978-1-7283-8692-8 (sc)
ISBN: 978-1-7283-8693-5 (hc)
ISBN: 978-1-7283-8691-1 (e)

Print information available on the last page.

Any people depicted in stock imagery provided by Getty Images are models,
and such images are being used for illustrative purposes only.
Certain stock imagery © Getty Images.

This book is printed on acid-free paper.

# Acknowledgements

I would like to thank all members of the Muchena family and friends for their support during the period of research and writing of this book. I would like to acknowledge also a number of people from whom I obtained various references, legislative documents, and other sources of information on the Angolan insurance market. My key contact persons were Alváro, António, Domingos, Firmino, Henda, Joaquim, Rajeev, Rolande, and Talent. I am also very grateful for the assistance I received from Ashley and Sabrina in Mauritius as well as my former colleagues in the African Reinsurance Corporation. I would like to thank Professor Richard Haines and other staff members in the Development Studies Group at the Nelson Mandela Metropolitan University, South Africa. Some of the ideas shared in this book were informed by insights from my studies on theory, policy, and practice of development with this group.

Furthermore, I would like to thank the executive management of Hollard Insurance Company of South Africa and Hollard Moçambique Companhia de Seguros, which gave me an opportunity from 2006 to 2007 to work on a new business exploration project in Angola. Although we were not able eventually to secure an insurance license as per our plans, participating in this business venture gave me an opportunity to start learning about insurance in Angola and develop a network of contacts there. Some of the people I met during this period were among my sources for updated information on key developments in this market as I was preparing to publish this case study.

In addition, I had opportunities to refine many of the ideas covered in this book through participation in a number of conferences on insurance and microinsurance in Abuja, Accra, Colombo, Dakar, Frankfurt, Harare, Khartoum, Lagos, Lusaka, Kigali, Maputo, Paris, Port Louis, and Victoria

Falls. I would like to acknowledge the organisations that facilitated my participation in these events, including the Access to Insurance Initiative (A2ii), the African Insurance Organisation (AIO), the African Management Services Company (AMSCO), the African Development Bank (AfDB), the African Reinsurance Corporation, the African Risk Capacity (ARC), the Centre for Financial Regulation and Inclusion (CENFRI), Enhancing Financial Innovation & Access (EFInA), the Global Index Insurance Facility (GIIF), the German development agency *Deutsche Gesellschaft für Internationale Zusammenarbeit* (*GIZ*), the International Finance Corporation (IFC), FinMark Trust, the Insurance Institute of Mauritius (IIM), the International Labour Organisation (ILO), and the Organisation of Eastern and Southern Africa Insurers (OESAI).

Finally, I would like to thank you the reader for the opportunity to present my review of the history of development of this key frontier insurance market. I am keen to engage in further discussions on the themes covered in this case study on the development of insurance in Angola and in other African countries as I prepare for the next market research project.

# Contents

# Frequently Asked Questions

## Emergence of Insurance in Angola

## Social Insurance and Public Funds

## Key Conditions for Setting Up and Running an Insurance Company

## Intermediation of Insurance and Reinsurance

## Obligatory Private Insurance

## Obligatory Coinsurance

# Reinsurance

# Insurance Contracts and Rating Guidelines

## Structure and Performance of the Emerging Insurance Market

## Legal Framework for Doing Business

# List of Tables

# List of Figures

# Acronyms

| | |
|---|---|
| AGT | Administração Geral Tributária (General Tax Administration) |
| AOA | Angolan Kwanza (International Code) |
| AML/CFT | Anti-money-laundering and combating the financing of terrorism |
| AMSA | Associação de Mediadores de Seguros de Angola (Association of Insurance Intermediaries of Angola) |
| AIPEX[1] | Agência de Investimento Privado e Promoção das Exportações (Agency for Private Investment and Promotion of Exports) |
| APIEX | Agência para a Promoção do Investimento e Exportações (Agency for the Promotion of Investment and Exports) |
| ARSEG | Agência Angolana de Regulação e Supervisão de Seguros (Insurance Regulatory and Supervisory Authority of Angola) |
| art. | article (*artigo*) |
| ASAN | Associação de Seguradoras de Angola (Association of Insurers of Angola) |
| ASEL | Associação de Supervisores de Seguros Lusófonos (Portuguese-speaking Markets Insurance Association) |
| ATI | African Trade Insurance Agency |
| BODIVA | Bolsa de Dívida e Valores de Angola, SA (Debt and Stock Exchange of Angola) |

---

[1] AIPEX was formed in 2018 to replace the entity APIEX

| | |
|---|---|
| CCISA | Comissão de Coordenação da Indústria Seguradora de Angola (Coordinating Committee of the Insurance Industry of Angola) |
| ch. | chapter (*capítulo*) |
| CISNA | Committee of Insurance, Securities, and Non-Banking Financial Authorities |
| cl. | clause |
| CNAIL | Comissão Nacional de Avaliação de Incapacidades Laborais (National Commission for Assessment of Occupational Disabilities) |
| CPAT | Comissão de Prevenção de Acidentes de Trabalho (Work Accident Prevention Committees) |
| CTSFP | Conselho Técnico de Seguros e Fundos de Pensões (Technical Council of Insurance and Pension Funds) |
| CPLP | Comunidade dos Países de Língua Portuguesa (Community of Portuguese Language Countries) |
| ENSA | Empresa Nacional de Seguros de Angola (National Insurance Company of Angola) |
| FATCA | Foreign Account Tax Account Compliance Act |
| FDA | Fundo de Garantia Automóvel (Motor Insurance Guarantee Fund) |
| FUNDAP | Fundo de Actualização das Pensões de Acidentes de Trabalho e Doenças Profissionais (Fund for Actualisation of Pensions of Workmen's Accident and Occupational Illnesses) |
| FUNSEG | Fundo de Actualização e Regularização de Seguros (Insurance Guarantee Fund) |
| GAAP | generally accepted accounting principles |
| IAIS | International Association of Insurance Supervisors |
| IFRS | International Financial Reporting Standards |
| IMO | International Maritime Organization |
| INSS | Instituto Nacional da Segurança Social (National Social Security Institute) |
| IOPS | International Organisation of Pension Supervisors |

| | |
|---|---|
| ISS | Instituto de Supervisão de Seguros (Insurance Supervisory Body) |
| Kz | Angolan Kwanza (symbol) |
| MCR | minimum capital required |
| PALOP | Países Africanos de Língua Oficial Portuguesa (Portuguese-speaking African Countries) |
| s. | section (*secção*) |
| SA | Sociedade Anónima (Public limited liability company/ joint-stock company) |
| SADC | Southern African Development Community |
| SGMR | Sociedade Gestora de Mercados Regulamentados (Management Company of Regulated Markets) |
| sub-s. | subsection (sub-secção) |
| TNI | Tabela Nacional de Incapacidade (National Disability Table) |

# Foreword

I congratulate Mr. Israel Muchena on such a laudable achievement and contribution to the development of insurance business in Angola and by extension the African continent.

Historically speaking, an important milestone in the development of the Angolan Insurance market was on the 18th day of May 1991, when the Peoples Republic of Angola, passed into law Resolution no. 10/91 allowing the country to become a shareholder of the African Reinsurance Corporation.

With premium income of more than US$ 1 billion, Angola is among the top 10 insurance markets in Africa. Currently, oil and gas insurance business represents the bulk of premium from this market. Given limited local underwriting capacity of the dominant oil and gas risks, the Angolan insurance market relies significantly on regional and international reinsurance markets.

As outlined in this book, there are also efforts by Angolan policymakers to create local reinsurance capacity. Africa Re is willing to assist in this initiative by providing additional capacity that may be required through two outlets; namely, Africa Re as a Corporation, and the African Oil & Energy Pool which it managers on behalf of African insurance companies.

Notwithstanding the large size of the Angolan insurance market, there is still a largely untapped potential in many segments of this market. Like several of its African counterparts, the Angolan insurance market despite its oil income still has an insurance market penetration of less than 1%. The main areas with growth potentials are life, personal lines, agriculture and small enterprises. The writer provides insights which highlight some of the critical policy measures that could be considered for inclusive growth and development of insurance in Angola.

Furthermore, this book comes at an opportune time given that the Angolan authorities are planning to carry out a comprehensive review of the current insurance legislation. Issues raised herein should assist in modernizing the insurance regulatory framework, as part of a broader strategy to develop the non-oil sector and diversify the economy.

Another interesting point is that the book breaks new ground by presenting information on this Lusophone market in English rather than Portuguese language, thereby targeting a wider audience.

It is also worthy of note that this is not the first from the stable of Mr. Israel Muchena as he also published *Development of Insurance in Mozambique*, in 2017. He was awarded the prize of the Book of the Year by the African Insurance Organisation for his effort, later that year. Israel has published several articles and presented a number of papers in several regional and international conferences on insurance, microinsurance and reinsurance.

Finally, it is hoped that others will follow in the footsteps of Israel Muchena in researching, writing and producing quality articles and publications on different topical aspects of insurance and reinsurance business in Africa.

**Corneille Karekezi**
**Group Managing Director/ Chief Executive Officer**
**African Reinsurance Corporation**

# Preface

The Sigma Report no. 2/2016 of the Swiss Reinsurance Company identified Angola as one of the key frontier insurance markets in Africa. The report defined as *frontier insurance markets* countries that had a significant potential for growth in the future. The markets in question had very low penetration rates of insurance compared to global standards. The report observed that insurance business in these countries, including Angola, would 'take off' and 'catch up' with the continued significant growth that was expected in these economies. Our study identified the insurance regulatory framework as one of the critical enabling factors for the development of insurance. We have reviewed all key aspects of the current insurance legal framework of Angola in this book and highlighted areas that we believed could be improved.

This case study was also a continuation of the type of work we started with the publication of *Development of Insurance in Mozambique* in 2016. It was part of our effort to contribute to the discussion on the kind and nature of development policies in African insurance markets. We shall not review the principles and practice of insurance. We are targeting readers who have some prior knowledge of the theory and practice of insurance.

Furthermore, we would like to note that in our review of the different pieces of law of interest, we placed more emphasis on presenting our understanding than on providing direct translations from Portuguese to English of every single word in the relevant legal conditions. We shall also not discuss all the clauses in all the legislation of interest. For people who might want to learn more about the legal conditions for doing insurance business in Angola, we recommend further review of appropriate legislation. We shall present the key identified items in the law in the form of frequently asked questions. We have put the full list of questions at the beginning of the book with the page numbers where the answers can be located.

# Chapter 1

# BACKGROUND INFORMATION

Before beginning our review of the development of insurance in Angola, we will briefly discuss the geography, history, and economy of this country. Angola is located in south-western Africa. It shares borders with Namibia in the south, Zambia in the east, and the Democratic Republic of Congo in the east and north. To the west, it faces the Atlantic Ocean, with a shoreline of 1,600 kilometres. At the time of writing this book, this territory, covering a total area of 1,246,700 square kilometres, had a population of only 25 million people. It was the seventh-largest country in Africa and had one of the lowest population densities on the continent.

Angola is also abundantly endowed with natural resources, including oil, diamonds, iron ore, manganese, bauxite, uranium, phosphates, and copper. Additionally, according to the World Energy Council, Angola has one of the highest hydropower potentials in Africa.[2] However, as of this writing, only a small portion of that potential has been explored.

**Figure 1: Map of Angola**

Source: Burmesedays—own work based on the Perry-Castañeda Library Map Collection Angola Maps, CC BY 3.0, https://commons.wikimedia. org/w/index.php?curid=22742968.

---

[2] . As noted on the web site of the World Energy Council, https://www.worldenergy. org/data/resources/country/angola/hydropower/ (accessed 30 June 2018).

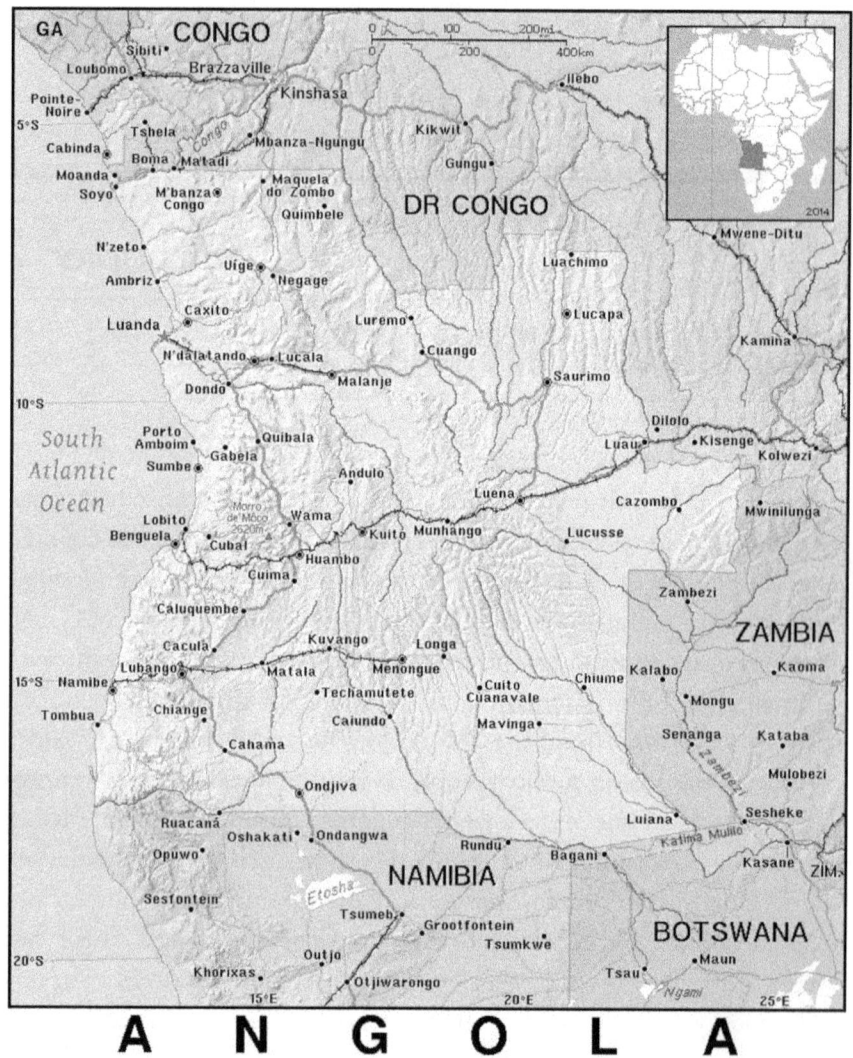

## 1.1 HISTORY OF ANGOLA

At the time of our research for this book, it was believed that the San people were the first inhabitants of the territory now known as Angola. During the first millennium AD, the San were displaced by the Bantu people (Warner, 1991: 5). The name of the country was derived from the word *ngola*, which means "king" in Kimbundu, one of the main

2

indigenous languages in this country. Kimbundu was part of the Bantu group of languages spoken in central, south-east, and southern Africa.

The Portuguese explorer Diogo Cáo was the first known European to make contact with Angola, which he did in 1484. This was followed by the first Portuguese settlements in Luanda in 1557. In the early days of exploration of Angola, the main interest of the Portuguese was trade in slaves to work in plantations in São Tomé e Príncipe and Brazil (Reader, 1998: 371). Portugal began to further develop the colonial economy of Angola and her other interests in Africa following the partitioning of the continent at the Berlin Conference of 1884–85.

The Angolan War of Independence began in 1961 as a revolt of the indigenous population against the colonial system of forced labour on cotton plantations (Warner, 1991: 28). Angola attained independence on 11 November 1975. According to Shillington (2005: 406), soon after gaining independence, Angola descended into a civil war (1975–2002) between two of the former liberation movements, the Movimento Popular para a Libertação de Angola (MPLA) and União Nacional para a Independência Total de Angola (UNITA). By the time of the final ceasefire in April 2002, it had become the longest and one of the most destructive wars in Africa.

## 1.2 MEMBERSHIP OF PALOP AND CPLP

Following the historical background outlined above, we note that the use of Portuguese as the official language of Angola was one of the principal legacies from the period when the country was a colony of the Portuguese empire. Angola was part of a community of five Portuguese-speaking countries in Africa referred to in Portuguese as Países Africanos de Língua Oficial Portuguesa (PALOP). Besides Angola, the other PALOP countries were Cape Verde, Guinea-Bissau, Mozambique, and São Tomé e Príncipe. Furthermore, Angola and the other PALOP countries were part of a broader global grouping of Portuguese-speaking countries known as the Comunidade dos Países de Língua Portuguesa (CPLP). The member countries of this community were as shown in Figure 2.

**Figure 2: Map of Portuguese-Speaking Countries**

Source: http://albertohelder.blogspot.com/2013/08/lusofonia-ranking-das-seleccoes.html.

# 1.3 NATURAL HAZARDS PROFILE

Angola had a low natural risks exposure. Flooding, drought, and landslides were the main natural perils to which the territory was exposed. According to the United Nations International Strategy for Disaster Reduction (UNISDR, 2015), the ranking of frequency of natural hazards exposure for Angola in the period 1990–2014 was as shown in Figure 3. Droughts were the most critical natural risk. However, this risk had no impact on the traditional insurance market, since there were no insurers actively exploring agriculture insurance. We were aware that the ENSA, the public insurer, was exploring prospects of launching weather index insurance products in the market in partnership with appropriate authorities (AngoNotícias, 2018).

**Figure 3: Major Natural Hazards Exposure of Angola**

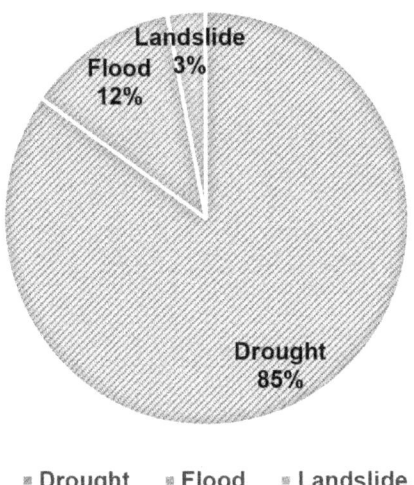

1.4 ECONOMY OF ANGOLA

Forty years of fighting during the struggle for independence and the post-independence civil war severely disrupted development of the Angolan economy. In addition, a significant portion of economic resources was spent on the war effort. While the ruling party relied on oil revenue to finance the war, the rebel movement had access to diamonds. Following a realization by Angolan policymakers that central planning limited economic development—and with the beginning of collapse of communism in the Soviet Union and Eastern Europe—the government of Angola initiated plans for economic reforms beginning in 1987 (Ferreira, 2006: 25). To support this exercise, the Angolan parliament passed the Constitutional Reform Law of 16 September 1992. The revised constitution paved the way for, among other things, adoption of a market-based national economic policy. This shift of the national economic policy also had a direct impact on the structure of the insurance market, as we will discuss in the next chapter.

Following the end of the civil war and the opening of the economy, Angola experienced a golden age of economic growth in the period 2002–2008 (da Rocha, 2012: 1). Angola attained an average annual growth rate of 14.9 per cent in this period. This impressive economic growth rate could be attributed mainly to the rise of oil prices from $52.60 per barrel in 2002 to $93.70 per barrel in 2008. However, this growth trend was not sustained in the periods that followed up to 2017, as shown in Figure 4.

**Figure 4: Angolan GDP from 1990 to 2017 (Billions of US dollars)**

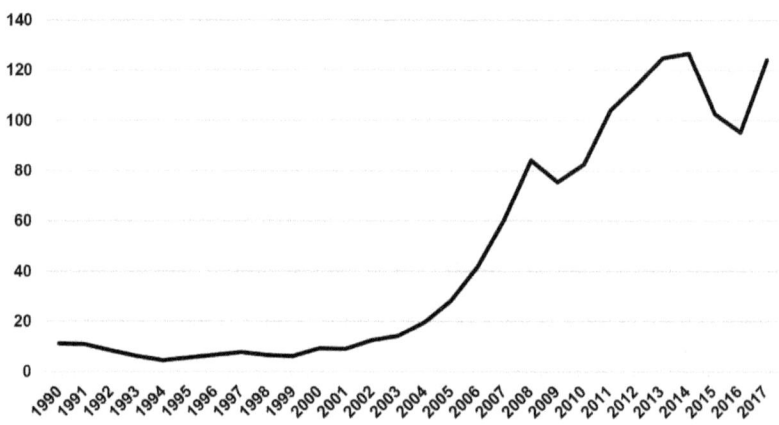

Given the negative impact of fluctuating oil prices, the principal preoccupation of Angolan policymakers was to reduce excessive dependence on this sector. Sharp reductions of oil prices adversely affected economic performance, given that this sector represented 30 per cent of the GDP and produced 95 per cent of export revenue for the country (Muzima and Gallardo, 2017: 243). The government implemented measures aimed at reducing oil price shocks, including the following:

- rationalisation of public expenditure through reduction of fuel subsidies
- implementation of policies aimed at stimulating non-oil activities
- shifting foreign exchange policy from a fixed exchange rate to a more market-oriented system

Angolan policymakers decided to abandon the fixed exchange rate system in order to 'improve foreign currency supply in the economy' (FocusEconomics, 2018: 1). In our review of the performance of the exchange rate of the Angolan Kwanza in the primary exchange rate market, as presented on the website of Banco Nacional de Angola,[3] we noted a sharp drop in the value of the local currency in the first quarter of 2018, as illustrated in Figure 5. Following these measures, we observed that there was an easing of the crisis and an improved availability of foreign exchange for various transactions, including funds for foreign reinsurance premium remittances.

**Figure 5: Exchange Rate of the Kwanza to the US Dollar**

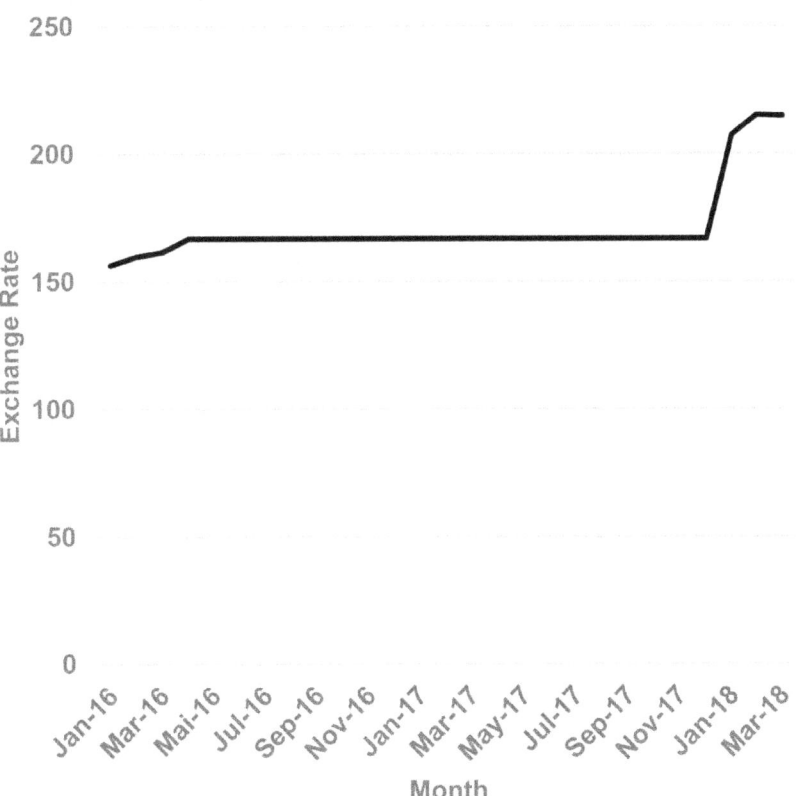

Following this major shift of foreign exchange policy and other measures adopted by the government, Fitch, the international rating agency, announced an upgrading of the outlook for Angola for its B rating

---

[3] . As per the website of Banco Nacional de Angola, http://www.bna.ao/Conteudos/ Artigos/lista_artigos_medias.aspx?idc=161&idsc=223&idl=1 (accessed 1 May 2018).

from negative to stable (Bordalo, 2018). 'Stable outlook' meant that Angola had a chance to upgrade from a junk investment category (B–, B, B+) to medium investment risk (BBB–, BBB, BBB+). This improvement of the sovereign rating of Angola was important because sovereign rating affects the rating of financial companies operating in that territory.

After the post-war transition described earlier, some observers were of the view that Angola's was a 'pre-emerging' economy (da Conceição, 2016: 13). Notwithstanding the natural wealth of Angola, it had been classified as one of the least developed countries since 1994. This was a category of low-income countries that faced severe 'structural impediments to sustainable development.' Angola had been found to have one of the most difficult environments for doing business in the world (The Heritage Foundation, 2018: 79). We discuss some of these challenges in this book for business in general and insurance activity in particular.

In view of the challenges noted, Angolan policymakers started implementing measures aimed at addressing the problems limiting the country's development prospects. Although the Angolan government was not accessing any loans from the International Monetary Fund (IMF), policymakers decided to seek technical support from this international institution through the Policy Coordination Instrument (Novo Jornal, 2018a). According to a UN resolution passed in 2016, Angola was expected to graduate to a 'Middle Income Country' by 2021 (UN, 2016). Angola was also upgraded to the category of Middle Human Development Indices and Indicators report of the UNDP (2018: 24).

## 1.5 FRONTIER INSURANCE MARKETS

We were aware that Angola had been ranked as one of the key emerging frontier insurance markets in Africa (Swiss Re, 2016). Key frontier markets identified in this study were those countries with a low penetration rate of insurance but with potential for significant growth in insurance and other financial services following continued economic growth. As presented in this study, the key macroeconomic indicators and performance of the insurance sector of Angola and other frontier markets in Africa were as summarized in Table 1.

**Table 1: Sub-Saharan Africa Frontier Insurance Markets**

| Country | GDP US$ Billion | GDP Capita US$ | GDP Growth (2016- 20) | Population in Millions | Non- Life % of GDP | Life % of GDP | Total Insurance % of GDP |
|---------|------|------|------|------|------|------|------|
| Angola | 126 | 5,038 | 3.9% | 25.0 | 0.98% | 0.02% | 1.00% |
| Côte d'Ivoire | 30 | 1,308 | 6.7% | 22.7 | 0.87% | 0.75% | 1.62% |
| Ethiopia | 58 | 583 | 6.5% | 99.4 | 0.57% | 0.04% | 0.62% |
| Ghana | 39 | 1,412 | 6.0% | 27.4 | 0.57% | 0.51% | 1.07% |
| Kenya | 64 | 1,381 | 6.2% | 46.1 | 1.91% | 1.07% | 2.98% |
| Mozambique | 22 | 794 | 6.7% | 28.0 | 1.05% | 0.18% | 1.23% |
| Nigeria | 502 | 2,753 | 5.0% | 182.2 | 0.21% | 0.08% | 0.29% |

Source: Swiss Re, Sigma No. 2/2016: 6

Furthermore, we observed that the insurance market of Angola had rapidly expanded from one monopoly insurer at the beginning of 2001 to twenty-seven registered insurers by the end of November 2018. The names of the registered insurers and year of formation are outlined in Appendix I. We should note that some of the registered licenses were dormant or never became operational. We shall discuss the state of the insurance market in Chapter 13.

# References

AngoNotícias (2018), 'ENSA Lança Seguro Agrícola', *Jornal Mercado*, 27/06/2018, http://www.angonoticias.com/Artigos/item/58316/ensa-lanca-seguro-agricola (accessed 30 June 2018).

Bordalo, Ricardo (2018), 'FMI e Governo Definem Metas para a Assistência Técnica a Angola', *Novo Jornal*, http://www.novojornal.co.ao/economia /interior/fmi-e-governo-definem-metas-para-a-assistencia-tecnica-a-angola---medidas-severas-em-perspectiva-57174.html?utm_term= Bom+dia%2C+sim.+-+Newsletter+Novo+Jornal&utm_campaign= Newsletters&utm_source=e-goi&utm_medium=email (accessed on 6 August 2018).

da Conceião, Alcino Izata (2016), *Angola no Contexto Financeiro Global*, Luanda–Mayamba Editora.

da Rocha, Alves (2012), 'Economic Growth in Angola to 2017 – The Main Challenges', Angola Brief, December 2012, vol. 2 no. 4, Centro de Estudo e a Investigação Científica – Universidade Católica de Angola & CMI (Chr. Michelsen Institute).

Ferreira, Manuel Ennes (2006), 'Angola: Conflict and Development, 1961-2002', *The Economics of Peace and Security Journal*, vol. 1, www. epsjournal.org.uk.

Ferreira, Monteiro, Rolando (1966), 'Como e Seguro Nasceu.' *Seguros: Série Técnica*, no. 114, December 1966; 121–123. Lisboa: Largo do Intendente Pina Manique.

Focus Economics (2018), 'Angola Economic Outlook', 20/03/2018 on the website https://www.focus-economics.com/countries/angola

Muzima, Joel, and Glenda Galardo (2017), 'Country Notes - Angola 2017', *African Economic Outlook* 2017, AfDB, OECD, and UNDP.

Novo Jornal (2018). 'Primeira consequência da "chegada do FMI foi no "rating" do pais, Fitch passa Angola de perspectiva negativa para estável', 26/04/2018: http://www.novojornal.co.ao/economia/interior/primeira-consequencia-da-chegada-do-fmi-foi-no-rating-do-pawas-fitch-passa-angola-de-perspectiva-negativa-para-estavel-52890.html?utm_term=Bom+dia%2C+sim.+-+Newsletter+Novo+Jornal&utm_campaign=Newsletters&utm_source=e-goi&utm_medium=email

Reader, J. (1998), *Africa: A Biography of the Continent*. London: Penguin Books, 371.

Shillington, K. (2005), *History of Africa*. New York: Palgrave Macmillan.

Swiss Re (2016), 'Insuring the Frontier Markets', *Sigma*, no. 2/2016. Zurich: Swiss Reinsurance Company Ltd.

The Heritage Foundation (2018), 'Index of Economic Freedom', as accessed at https://www.heritage.org/index/pdf/2018/countries/angola.pdf on 25/04/2018.

UN (2016), 'Graduation of Angola from the Least Developed Country Category', UN General Assembly Resolution A/RES/70/253, adopted on 12 February 2016.

UNDP (2018), 'Human Development Indices and Indicators', 2018 Statistical Upgrade. New York: United Nations Development Programme.

UNISDR (2015), Angola Disaster and Risk Profile, https://www.preventionweb.net/countries/ago/data/ (accessed on 30/06/2018).

Warner, Rachel (1991), Historical Setting. In T. Collelo (ed) *Angola: A Country Study*, ed. Thomas Collelo. Washington: Library of Congress, 5–50.

Chapter 2

# HISTORY OF INSURANCE AND EMERGENCE IN ANGOLA

*History does not necessarily limit the possibility or probability of acts or thoughts in the past. History merely is a limit in our knowledge to a specific point in the past.*

—*Robert Secovnie*

Following our review of the history, geography and economy of Angola, we shall now discuss the origins of insurance in Asia and Europe and its advent in Africa, including Angola. In alignment with the quotation above from Robert Secovnie, we were aware that our knowledge of ancient mechanisms of coping with risk among the earliest settlers in the territory now known as Angola was very limited. As in ancient Asian and European civilizations, the Bantu people in Africa had their own traditional ways of coping with risk. It was believed that these risk-related customs predated the insurance practice that was introduced to Africa by European settlers in the twentieth century. Following adoption of the conventional form of insurance business worldwide, insurance had developed into an 'indispensable' business activity to provide protection against 'the inherent uncertainties of human life' (Prudential Insurance Company, 1915: 3). The history of development of insurance was closely intertwined with 'human progress.'

## 2.1 ORIGINS OF RISK

According to Vaughan (1992: 3), risk is a 'pervasive condition of human existence'. In alignment with this perspective, risk has always been present, from the beginning of existence of mankind. There always existed a possibility that our experience of the future would not be in accordance with our current expectations. There was always a chance that not everything would go according to plan based on our knowledge of the current state of affairs. It was in accordance with this that one could assert that nobody could 'escape risk' (Holmes, 2004: 1).

Other insurance analysts saw the biblical story of Noah, the ark, and the flood (Genesis 6–9) as a clear presentation of a problem of risk and the planning and handling of risk. In this story, the work of Noah to save lives in the face of a major natural catastrophe could be seen as one of the earliest examples of risk management. He invested in a plan to save lives in anticipation of major flooding. He realized that the event could not be prevented or avoided. The physical risk-control measures he implemented in building the ark were intended to mitigate the impact of the flooding. We should now review briefly the formal history of the development of insurance as one of the mechanisms for coping with risk.

## 2.2 FIVE THOUSAND YEARS OF INSURANCE

At the time of writing this book, it is widely believed that the business activity of insurance developed over a period of five millennia. We noted key dates and periods in the timeline of the insurance networking event known as Operational Excellence Insurance.[4] We shall not discuss all the milestones in the development of insurance. We shall focus only on few key stages of development of insurance as outlined in Table 2.

---

[4] .Operational Excellence Insurance as per the website: https://www.operationalexcellenceinsurance.com/downloads/infographic-a-history-of-insurance-timeline?-ty-m (accessed on 03/01/2018).

## Table 2: Timeline of Ancient History of Insurance

| Period | Historical Development |
|--------|------------------------|
| 3000 BC | Risk-sharing among Chinese merchants |
| 2000 BC | Hammurabi Code in Mesopotamia |
| 1000 BC | Creation of the concept of contribution on the island of Rhodes |
| 700 BC | Embryonic forms of insurance in sacred Hindu writings, including Law of Manu |
| 300 BC | Bottomry contracts of Phoenician and Greek traders |
| 200 BC | Mutual fund arrangements of Achaemenia |

## Apportionment of Risk by Chinese Merchants

The oldest signs of insurance-related practices can be traced back to the period 5000–2300 BC (Nascimento, 2015). According to ancient records of China from this period, merchants developed a mechanism to share burdens of misfortunes in their business of transporting goods by boat. The merchants were at risk of financial ruin after accidents in 'treacherous rapids' along the rivers in their voyages. In order to protect themselves, they adopted a practice of sharing risks. They would distribute commodities of each merchant in many boats in order to limit the amount that could be lost by any one of them in case of loss of any one of the boats during the journey.

With this risk-sharing mechanism, if one of the boats was lost, all the members of the group would suffer only a small loss, for only part of their cargo was on the boat affected by the misfortune. The principal underlying concept in this ancient practice—a spreading of the costs of a few among many people—remains a key pillar of universal insurance business models.

## Hammurabi Code

The most ancient recording of an insurance agreement is part of the oldest form of a written law known as the Hammurabi Code from 2000 BC (Vaughan, 1992: 63). Merchants of the Babylonian kingdom in ancient Mesopotamia followed this ancient law. As part of key business practices of the period, hawkers or traders would be hired to sell commodities in the kingdom and neighbouring territories. In order to secure loans to do their business, these hawkers, known as *darmatha*, would pledge their belongings, including 'property, wife and children'. Unfortunately, many of the traders would lose their possessions due to the growing problem of robberies on their trade routes. Following a revolt of traders who had suffered many losses, the traders agreed to have what could be viewed as the first form of an 'insurance contract' as part of the ancient legal system of the Code (Mehr and Cammack, 1972: 744).

## Development of the Principle of Contribution on the Island of Rhodes

According to a publication of Prudential Insurance Company of America (1915: 5), the principle of contribution was developed in the Sea Law of the Island of Rhodes in 1000 BC. The law stated that '… if goods were thrown overboard in order to lighten the ship, what was sacrificed for the common benefit should be made good by a common contribution.' Storms represented one of the biggest perils of loss, and if the captain found it necessary to throw out into the sea some of the cargo in order to save the ship, it was believed to be fair for the owners of the cargo sacrificed to suffer such a loss on their own. In accordance with the regulations of the Rhodian Law on the liability of such lost or damaged goods, the costs were to be shared between the shipowner, other cargo owners, and passengers saved from the event. This ancient principle of contribution is maintained in current marine insurance contracts.

## Pooling of Resources in Ancient Sacred Hindu Text

Ancient sacred Hindu texts describe early forms of insurance in India from approximately 700 BC (Nascimento, 2015). The writings of Manusmrithi or Laws of Manu and the other texts of this period refer to a practice of 'pooling of resources' that would be shared in periods of disaster, such as 'fire, floods, epidemics and famine' (IRDA, 2017). The concept of pooling of risks has been maintained in modern-day insurance as one mechanism of handling of risks.

## Bottomry Contracts

The next phase in early forms of insurance contracts were the bottomry contracts developed by Phoenician and Greek traders (Mehr and Cammack, 1972: 744). These were contracts in which shipowners would borrow money to equip or repair a ship using the vessel itself as collateral. It would be stipulated in the bottomry contract that if the ship were to be lost during the covered voyage or period as a result of covered perils, the loan could be cancelled (Irukwu 1998: 6). The loan was supposed to be collected only if the ship survived the covered voyage or period. For this type of contract, the lender would charge a higher interest rate than the standard for this risk carried by the lender. We are aware that practice of bottomry contracts had become obsolete at the time of writing this book.

## Mutual Funds in Guild Systems

The next key milestone in the history of insurance involved insurance-related activities in guild systems of the dark and middle ages. In that period, a master would train young men joining societies or guilds to become artisans. In exchange for regular contributions, the members of the guild would enjoy benefits such as a form of funeral coverage. In the same period, rulers of ancient Iranian kingdoms known as the Achaemenian monarchs were practicing basic types of mutual fund arrangements. At the beginning of each year, the subjects would donate part of their harvest to the rulers. Then, in the event of misfortunes, the rulers would assist them. We should note that in the earliest forms of insurance described above, the activity of assuming risk was not an autonomous business (Waty, 2007: 8).

# 2.3 MEDIEVAL AND EARLY MODERN

**Table 3: Key Developments in the Medieval and Early Modern Epoch**

| Period | Historical Development |
| --- | --- |
| 1343 | Oldest recorded insurance contract in Genoa |
| 1552 | Publishing of the first book on insurance, *On Insurance and Merchants' Bets* by Pedro Santarém (Santerna) |

| 1654 | Gambler's debate leading to creation of mathematical theory of probability |
|---|---|
| 1666 | The Great Fire of London |
| 1667–81 | Nicholas Barbon established the first insurance office in London |
| 1688 | Formation of Lloyds' |
| 1693 | Edmond Halley develops the first mortality table |

## Separate Insurance Agreements

As part of the next stage in the development of insurance, there emerged in Genoa in the fourteenth century the first form of insurance contracts as separate agreements not combined with other business. This development of separate insurance agreements also became a key feature of modern-day insurance. The approach of bundling insurance with other transactions was also maintained in areas such as Bancassurance. We also noted an emerging trend where insurance supervisors were concerned about practices of conditional selling associated with bundling of insurance with other transactions.

## Formulation of Probability Theory and Development of Mortality Tables

The next key development in the mathematical concepts underpinning insurance came in 1654 with the creation of the theory of probability following a debate on the principles of chance that could be deduced from a popular game of dice. The debate was between two famous French mathematicians: Blaise Pascal and Pierre de Fermat (Bernstein, 1996: 3). After the theory of probability was formulated and refined, it was applied in a number of fields, including insurance. In insurance, probability was the mathematical basis on which risk was calculated (IISA, 2011: 127, and Hafeman, 2009: 2). Some of the key technical terms used in insurance originated from gambling, the basis on which probability was developed. For instance, the word *risk* was derived from the early Italian word *riscare*, which meant 'to dare'. *Hazard*, the other word used to refer to situations of risk covered by insurance, came from the Arabic word for dice: *al zahr* (Bernstein, 1996: 3).

Another key milestone based on the theory of probability was achieved in the same period with the construction of the first mortality tables (Ferreira, 1966: 123). These were a result of preliminary work from a study of demography of London by John Graunt and of the German town of Breslau by Caspar Neumann. Edmond Halley used this material to produce a mortality table that became a key reference for calculating premiums for life insurance (Ciecka, 2008: 65).

## Lloyd's of London

Following the historical events outlined above, the next stage of development in the insurance business was the emergence of marine insurance in London. Towards the end of the seventeenth century, with growing trade between European empires and the New World they were colonising, there was an increase of demand for marine insurance. This was followed by the emergence of the first insurance market. It started in the late 1680s in a coffee shop in London owned by a Mr Edward Lloyd. The shop became a popular meeting place for, on one hand, people wanting to insure ships and cargo, and on the other hand, those who wanted to provide such insurance. From that period, the place grew into the principal international market for financial and technical capacity to support insurance business worldwide. It was formally known as Lloyd's of London.

## Emergence of the Practice of Underwriting

Following the emergence of the first insurance market in London, a new profession of insurance began. In order to provide the service, people involved in this type of activity would, at first, negotiate and agree on terms and conditions of insurance with the merchants seeking it. After drafting a written agreement, the person assuming the responsibilities to make good on losses suffered by the merchants would sign underneath the written contract as part of the process of proof of insurance cover. This process of signing underneath the agreement would mark the beginning of the profession known as *underwriting*. The person signing would be referred to as the underwriter. On some insurance policies, there could be more than one underwriter assuming risk.

## The Insurance Institute of London

The activity described above developed from that period into a well-established formal profession. As one of the ways of gaining appropriate qualifications in this profession, one could enrol for training to become a chartered insurance practitioner. The Insurance Institute of London, formed in 1907, was the principal institution responsible for that training. There were affiliated or associated institutes in many countries worldwide, including Kenya, Malawi, South Africa, Zambia, and Zimbabwe in the southern Africa region. An equivalent entity did not exist in Angola.

## The Great Fire of London

Property insurance was the next step of development after marine insurance. This became a key area of focus following the Great Fire of London of September 1666 (Mehr and Cammack, 1972: 748). The fire destroyed most of the city and left many people without homes (Borscheid, 2013: 43). Following this tragic event, Dr Nicolas Barbon formed in 1680 the Fire Office, the first fire insurance company in the world (Vivian and Morgan, 2001: 21).

By the end of the seventeenth century, there were three fire offices in London. The next key areas of development were life and accidents insurance. We should now discuss key developments in Portugal, a country that would influence developments in Angola, amongst other countries in Africa.

## 2.4 THE PORTUGUESE EMPIRE AND GLOBAL EXPANSION

Companhia Permanente de Seguros, the first insurance company in Portugal, was formed in 1791 (Portugal, 2007: 13). Following this development, eight other insurers were set up in the same decade, followed by Companhia de Seguros Bonança at the beginning of the nineteenth century. From this period, Bonança would survive the longest in some form following acquisition by another insurance company. By the end of the nineteenth century, the emerging Portuguese insurance market would play a key role in other European markets in the expansion overseas into new markets, including Angola.

## 2.5 EXPANSION OF FORMAL INSURANCE TO AFRICA

Following the development of insurance in Europe, there was an expansion of insurance to other territories during the period of growth of world trade in the middle of the nineteenth century. Early insurers in Africa depended on traders as both clients of insurance and agents through which insurance could be arranged with other interested parties (Borscheid, 2013: 33). Insurers preferred to nominate trading firms as agents because they were well acquainted with the risks of shipment and storage of cargo. These were the most critical types of hazards for the fire and marine classes of insurance, which were the key types of insurance arranged in these new territories, including Angola.

## 2.6 ONE HUNDRED YEARS OF INSURANCE IN ANGOLA

The history of traditional risk-coping mechanisms in Angola is very similar to that of most countries in Africa. According to Irukwu (1998: 7), most African societies had basic forms of traditional social risk-sharing mechanisms that had been in existence before the formation of the contemporary insurance sector. These practices appear to have consisted mainly of some forms of mutual aid guarantees. Unfortunately, in Angola and other African countries, there were no known written historical records of such practices. Therefore, our review of the history of the development of insurance in Angola focused on the recorded history of insurance activities introduced by the Portuguese at the beginning of the twentieth century.

The developmental trajectory of the insurance market in Angola is similar in many ways to that of Mozambique, as described in our book *Development of Insurance in Mozambique* (Muchena, 2018). In a similar fashion to other African insurance markets, insurance started in Angola as part of the expansion of business activities from European colonial regimes (Nazaré, 2008: 71). From this period of emergence of insurance in Angola, the development of this business activity was strongly influenced by key shifts in the constitutional order and national political economy.

At the time of this writing, the development of the Angolan insurance market had gone through three key stages of development. The changes in the market followed key historical shifts in the constitutional law and the national political economy of Angola, as discussed below. The three key stages of development of this market can be summarised as shown in the outline in Figure 6.

**Figure 6: Key Stages of Development of the Angolan Market**

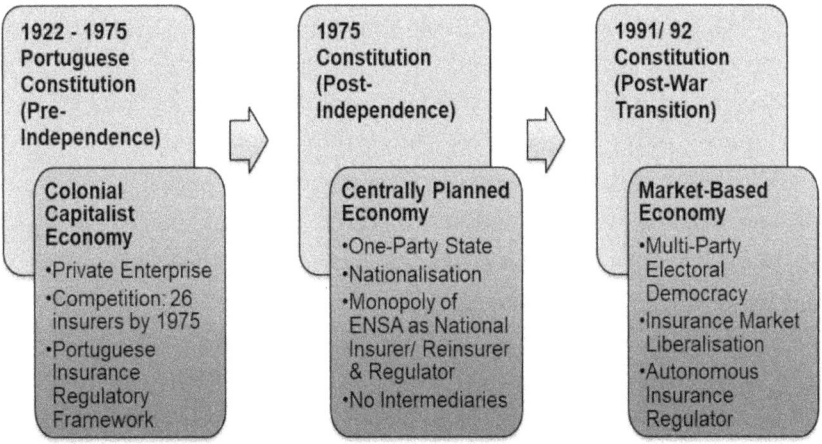

## 2.7 EARLY PHASE OF DEVELOPMENT: COLONIAL PERIOD

The first forms of insurance were general commercial enterprises that operated as insurance agents of insurers in Portugal. The Portuguese first arrived in Angola in 1483. Although the Portuguese initially showed little interest in this territory, that began to change following the process of partitioning of Africa at the Berlin Conference of 1884–85. In the early stages of the development of insurance in Angola, the nascent insurance markets in the colonies relied on the Portuguese insurance regulatory framework.

In Portugal, the central piece of insurance legislation at this time was the Decree of 21 October 1907.[5] We should note that this early insurance legislation referred already to the principle of separating life business from other types of insurance (ch. III, art. 28). In our opinion, this is one of the rules that we believe present-day Angolan policymakers should consider

---

[5] .Referred to in Portuguese as *Decreto de 21 de Outubro 1907—Das Condições do Exercício da Indústria Seguradora.*

reviewing, given that current insurance consists of composite insurance licenses. The emerging trend in global markets is for separation of life and non-life insurance licenses, operations, and management of companies.

Following an observation by the Portuguese government that there was an increasing number of requests for authorization by insurers to set up in the overseas colonies of Portugal, it was decided to establish legislation for the life insurance business in the colonies as per Decree no. 34,562 of 5 May 1945. As explained in the preamble of this regulatory legislation, the authorities were concerned about their ability to supervise operations of insurers far away. We shall discuss later in this book the key phases of the development of the insurance regulatory framework in Angola.

We shall not discuss in detail all the conditions specified in this first form of local insurance regulations in Angola. We would like to highlight a few of the key features of this legislation in respect to insurance companies registered in the colonies like Angola:

- Insurance companies were required to be public limited liability companies (ch. I, art. 2).
- At least 50 per cent of the specified minimum capital was supposed to be paid up (ch. I, art. 5, para. 1, cl. 3).
- Reinsurance placements were not subject to registration (ch. 1, art. 6).
- All rights and obligations arising from insurance contracts in the Portuguese Imperial Colony, including the overseas colonies like Angola, were subject to jurisdiction of Portuguese courts (ch. I, art. 9).

The same legislation provided legal provisions for registration and operation of agencies in the Portuguese colonies of insurance companies registered in Portugal (ch. III) or any other foreign country (ch. IV). The regulations in respect of this new regulatory framework were enacted through ordinance (*Portaria*) 7,895 of 31 July 1952 of the governor general of Angola at that time, José Agapito da Silva Carvalho.

## When was the first insurance company set up in Angola in the colonial period?

The first insurance company in Angola was set up in 1922 by Companhia de Seguros Ultramarina from Portugal (ARSEG, 2015: 12).

With the rapid growth of the Angolan economy in this period came an expansion of the insurance sector. The majority of the insurance groups that set up in Angola were from Portugal. When this emerging insurance market was at its peak in 1961, there were thirty insurance companies and one reinsurer (Nazaré, 2008: 78). However, by the time of independence, the number of operators had reduced to twenty-six companies, as shown in the list in Appendix II.

# 2.8 TRANSITION PERIOD

Angola attained its independence on 11 November 1975. As part of initiatives to address an emerging economic crisis during this period of change, the Ministry of Planning and Finance of the transitional government passed on 5 August 1975 decree no. 68/75. In this decree, the authorities created the coordinating committee of the insurance industry of Angola—Comissão de Coordenação da Indústria Seguradora de Angola or CCISA. (Nazaré, 2008: 81). As stipulated in the decree, the committee's responsibilities included coordinating and guiding the transformation of the insurance market in the post-independence period (art. 2).

What was the purpose of the national day of insurance?

Given the historical significance of the activities of the transitional committee, the date of its formation became a day for commemorating insurance. On 5 August each year, key stakeholders in the insurance market participated in events aimed at celebrating the National Day of Insurance and Pensions Funds (o Dia Nacional dos Seguros e Fundo de Pensões). The principal purpose of this day was to raise awareness of the need and benefits of insurance and pensions (Pinto, 2017). We did not find official reference to this commemoration event on the most recent legislation in respect of national public holidays and commemoration days, as defined in law no. 10/11 of 16 February 2011.

## What was the first insurer created in the post-independence period?

Following the passing of presidential decree no. 17/78 of 1 February 1978 in the transition period, a monopoly state-owned insurance and reinsurance company called Empresa Nacional de Seguros e Resseguros de Angola (ENSA) was established. The responsibilities of regulating and coordinating insurance business activities were transferred to ENSA following the termination of the respective transitional coordinating committee (CCISA) through decree no. 69-A/78 of 27 April 1978. These measures of creating a monopoly insurer were in alignment with the economic policy of centralized planning which had been adopted by the post-independence government.

The development initiatives of the post-independence government were disrupted by a highly destructive civil war that started soon after independence and only ended in 2002. As part of efforts to rehabilitate the war-ravaged economy, the Angolan government initiated a structural reform programme in 1987. This was followed by Law of Economic Activities no. 10/88 of 2 July 1988. This law paved the way for the termination of a state monopoly by creating space for individuals and legal business entities to do economic activities in areas not prohibited by law (Ch. I, art. 2). Up to this stage, the state played a central role in the planning of social and economic development activities of the country, as noted in the preamble of this law. With the new law, activities reserved exclusively for the state were reduced to key essential public services. As we shall discuss in Chapter 11, the policymakers continued to reduce the role of government in economic business activities with the new Private Investments Law no. 10/18 of 26 June 2018.

## When was there a shift from a monopoly to a competition-based market?

Starting in 1998, the government initiated measures to liberalize the insurance market and to create an autonomous insurance regulatory body (ARSEG, 2015: 13). The General Law of Insurance number 1/2000 was passed by the National Assembly of Angola on 3 February 2000. This law provided the principal piece of legislation for the operation of an insurance market based on competition. Towards the end of the same year, Sonangol, the national oil and gas parastatal, initiated the process of registering a second public insurer called AAA Seguros. This new company was registered first as a private limited-liability company on July 2000. Then, in order to ensure compliance with the new rules on the type of legal entity that could register as an insurer as defined in the new General Law of Insurance of 2000 (Ch. III, s. I, art. 13), the new insurer was registered as a public limited-liability company on 7 December 2000. The Sonangol group had total shareholding of 99.5 per cent in the new insurer (de Abreu, 2014: 349). AAA Seguros started its operations in 2001. Following this development, Nova Sociedade de Seguros de Angola, SA (NOSSA), the first privately owned insurer in Angola in the post-independence period, was authorised in 2004.

## 2.9 EVOLUTION OF INSURANCE REGULATORY FRAMEWORK

The development of an insurance regulatory body had accompanied the evolution of economic policies and constitutional order. Insurance regulatory framework has gone through the following three key phases of change:

1. 1922 to 1975—Portuguese insurance regulatory framework
2. 1978 to 2000—Self-regulation by ENSA, the monopoly insurance and reinsurance company
3. 2000 to date—autonomous regulatory body

In the first phases of Portuguese colonisation, the emerging insurance market in Angola relied on the insurance regulatory framework of Portugal. Then a local insurance regulatory entity referred to in Portuguese as Serviços de Fiscalização Técnica da Indústria Seguradora (SFTIS) was established in Angola and Mozambique through decree no. 37,076 of 29 September 1948 (de Abreu, 2014: 520). The new regulatory entity was authorised to charge a surtax of 0.5 per cent of insurance premiums from the insurance market. Next, authorities began a process of reform of the regulatory bodies in banking and insurance with the passing of decree no. 44702 of 17 November 1962 (Diário da República Electrónico). Following this legislation, there was formation of a new banking and insurance regulatory body, referred to in Portuguese as Inspecção de Crédito e Seguros (ICS). This process culminated in the formation of consultative organs in the regulatory body referred to as Conselhos Provinciais de Crédito e Seguros (CPCS), as constituted through decree no. 49304 of 16 October 1969.

## When was the insurance regulatory authority re-established?

Following plans to liberalise the economy, including the insurance market, the policymakers decided to re-establish an autonomous insurance regulatory body. The new body, known as Instituto de Supervisão de Seguros (ISS), was created through law no. 4/98 and the supporting regulations in decree no. 63/04 of 28 September 2004.

ISS was replaced in 2013 by the current insurance regulatory body, known as Agência Angolana de Regulação e Supervisão de Seguros (ARSEG). ARSEG was formed through presidential decree no. 141/13 of 27 September, 2013.[6] The new regulatory authority was intended to operate independently and was required to report to an independent board of directors. This approach of setting up of the regulatory body as an autonomous entity was in alignment with emerging global trends.

Furthermore, as we shall discuss in Chapter 4, in their plans to modernise the local regulatory framework, Angolan policymakers made reference to global standards from the International Association of Insurance Supervisors (IAIS) and other global organisations. Since the formation of IAIS in 1994, there had been cooperation in development of global guidelines for insurance regulators (Carmichael and Pormerleano, 2002: 85) as per international guidelines and a similar approach to what was adopted in countries such as Mozambique and South Africa. We have noted on the website of IAIS that Angola was not a member of this body.[7] At the time of writing this book, thirty-four African countries were members of IAIS (Africa Re, 2015: 12).

---

[6] .Referred to in Portuguese as *Decreto Presidencial nº 141/13 de 27 de Setembro*
[7] .See https://www.iawasweb.org/page/about-the-iais/iais-members, accessed 20/05/2018

## What were the rates of the annual levy payable to the insurance regulator?

According to the General Law of Insurance, the insurance regulator was supposed to have financial and administrative autonomy, as envisaged in ch. II, art. 11, cl. 2. In order for the regulatory body to attain this independence, it was entitled to collect an obligatory annual levy as specified in the Regulations on Conditions of Access and Conduct of Business of Insurers (ch. V, s. I, art. 14). The rates to be applied on the gross written premium net of reversals and cancellations were as follows:

- 0.2 per cent for life insurance
- 0.3 per cent for other insurance

We could not verify the budgets of the regulatory body because we could not locate its annual reports. We believe that in Angola and other African markets, there could be improved transparency.

## Does the insurance regulator have authority?

In our review of the regulatory framework, we noted that a significant amount of power and authority had been conferred on the insurance regulator. Through the sanctions regime, as defined in decree no. 7/02 of 9 April 2002, the regulator could apply fines and penalties on companies and individuals involved in all the segments of insurance business for failure to comply with the legal requirements. In addition, the regulator had authority to publish information on sanctions applied against operators in the insurance market in its informative publications, the Official Government Gazette (*Diário da República*), or a newspaper (ch. V, s. 1, art. 11). We believe that exposing repeat offenders or major compliance failures was a critical disincentive for entities in the insurance market to avoid adverse publicity. The regulator tended to defend the insurance market. We found that there was a school of thinking among some of the African insurance regulators that it was appropriate to avoid disclosing information that could trigger a loss of confidence in insurance.

Having discussed the sources of legislation in the insurance legal framework, we will move on in the next chapter to the insurance legislative framework of Angola.

# References

Africa Re (2015), *The African Insurance Regulatory Directory*, analysis prepared by Dr Schanz. Zurich: Alms and Company AG.

ARSEG (2015), *Desafios e Oportunidades—Estudo sobre o Sector Segurador e dos Fundos de Pensões em Angola*. Angola: PricewaterhouseCoopers Limitada.

Bernstein, P. L. (1996), *Against the Gods: the Remarkable Story of Risk*. New York: John Wiley

Borscheid, Peter (2013). 'Global Insurance Networks' in James, Harold (ed) *The Value of Risk: Swiss Re and the History of Reinsurance*. New York: Oxford University Press, 23–105.

Carmichael, J., and M. Pormerleano (2002), *The Development and Regulation of Non-Banking Financial Institutions*. Washington: The World Bank.

Ciecka, James, E. (2008), 'Edmond's Life Table and Its Uses', *Journal of Legal Economics*, vol. 15, no. 1: 65–74.

de Abreu, Ana Edith Viegas (2014), *100 Anos de Legislação de Seguros em Angola*. Luanda - Edições Chá de Caxinde.

*Diário da República Electrónica, Decreto-lei 44702, de 17 de Novembro,* https://dre.tretas.org/dre/259938/decreto-lei-44702-de-17-de-novembro (accessed 20 May 2018).

Ferreira, Monteiro Rolando (1966), 'Como e Seguro Nasceu', *Seguros*: Série Técnica. No. 114, December 1966. Lisboa: Largo do Intendente Pina Manique, 121–123.

Hafeman, Michael (2009), 'The Role of the Actuary in Insurance', *Primer Series on Insurance*, Issue 4, May 2009. Washington: The World Bank.

Holmes, Andrew (2004), *Smart Risk*, West Sussex: Capstone Publishing Limited.

IISA (2011), *Principles of Short Term Insurance*, Insurance Institute of South Africa.

IRDA (2017), History of Insurance in India, https://www.irdai.gov.in/ADMINCMS/cms/NormalData_Layout.aspx?page=PageNo4 &mid=2 (accessed on 15 June 2018).

Irukwu, J. O. (1998), *Insurance Management in Africa*, Lagos: BIMA Publications.

Mehr, Robert I., and Cammack, Emerson (1972), *Principles of Insurance*. Illinois: Richard D. Irwin, Inc.

Muchena, Israel (2018), *Development of Insurance in Mozambique*, Bloomington: AuthorHouse.

Nascimento, Luís (2015), *História do Seguro*, 4 November 2015, http://hwastoriadoseguro.com/sobre/ (accessed on 20 May 2018).

Nazaré, Domingas Miguel (2008), *A ENSA e a Reforma do Sector Seguradora em Angola*. Luanda–Caxinde: Editora e Livraria.

Pinto, Domingos (2017), *O Seguro proporciona "paz de espírito", bem-haja o 05 de Agosto*, Club-K Angola, 8 August 2017, http://www.club-k.net/index.php?option=com_content&view=article&id=28925:o-seguro-proporciona-paz-de-espirito-bem-haja-o-05-de-agosto-domingos-pinto&catid=17&lang=pt&Itemid=1067 (accessed on 20 May 2018).

Portugal, Luís (2007), *Gestão de Seguros Não-Vida*, Lisboa: Instituto de Formação Actuarial.

Prudential Insurance Company of America (1915), *The Documentary History of Insurance 1000 BC–1875 AD*. Newark: Prudential Press.

Secovnie, Robert (anon), *History of Insurance*. New York: Insurance Training Institute, http://iti-ny.com/H%20wastory%20of%20Insurance%20 11-1-16%20wpf%20(13)/HistoryofInsurance.pdf (accessed on 25 June 2018).

Vaughan, Emmet, J. (1992), *Fundamentals of Risk and Insurance*, 6th ed. New York: John Wiley and Sons Inc.

Vivian, Robert W., and Morgan, Jim (2001), *Morgan's History of the Insurance Institute Movement in South Africa*. Cape Town: Francolin Publishers.

Waty, Teodoro A. (2007), *Direito de Seguros*. M Maputo: W&W Editora Lda.

# Chapter 3

# INSURANCE LEGAL FRAMEWORK

Following our discussion of the emergence of insurance in Angola and the post-independence transition process, we shall now look at the current insurance legislation of Angola. As per the outline in Appendix III, we were able to track at least forty-seven pieces of current laws and regulations in respect of insurance. Some of the sources of the current insurance legislation in Angola dated from as far back as 130 years ago when Dom Luís, the king of Portugal, decreed the commercial code. We shall also review the financial institutions law, since it treated the insurance business as part of the non-banking category of financial services. In this case study, we shall refer to the financial sector legislation as well as the main insurance law and respective regulations as the insurance legal framework.

## 3.1 SOURCES OF LEGISLATION

Before discussing key pieces of the insurance legal framework, we should look at the sources of legislation in Angola. In accordance with the legal framework presented in a paper published by Rainha (2007), the order of the hierarchy of law in Angola was as follows:

1. Constitution law (*lei constitucional*) as the supreme law in Angola
2. Laws (*leis*) and resolutions (*resoluções*) passed by the National Parliament of Angola[8] as the principal legislative body on all matters except those reserved by the constitution to the government. We

---

[8] .Designated in Angola as *Assembleia Nacional*

should also note that some of the key legislation from the period when Angola was part of the Portuguese empire was still in force. Two such laws we shall discuss in this book were the Commercial Code of 1888 and the Civil Code originally passed in 1966.

3. Presidential decrees (*decretos presidenciais*) and presidential dispatches (*despachos presidenciais*)
4. Decree-laws (*decretos-leis*), decrees (*decretos*), and resolutions of the Council of Ministers (*Conselho de Ministros*)
5. Executive decree (*decreto executivo*) and legislative decree (*diploma ministerial*)
6. Circulars (*circulares*) and notices (*avisos*) which were formally enacted by the insurance regulatory body

We shall discuss some of the key legal rules and regulations at the different levels as provided for in these pieces of legislation.

## 3.2 COMMERCIAL CODE

Reference to foundational legal principles of insurance in the Angolan insurance regulatory framework were located in the Commercial Code (*Código Comercial*), as promulgated in the Charter (*Carta de Lei*) of 28 June 1888 (Achega, 2014: 585–593). The code, passed during the period when Angola was part of the Portuguese empire, was still in force at the time of writing this book. The legal conditions for insurance were defined in articles 425 to 462 of volume II, heading XV. In general, most of the legal conditions defined in this code were in accordance with the legal principles of insurance as first developed in English law and now accepted universally in all jurisdictions worldwide.

The legal principles of insurance and the legal elements of insurance contracts provided for in the Commercial Code were a key component of the legal foundations for the Insurance Contract Regulations (decree no. 2/02 of 11 February 2002), as we shall further review in Chapter 9. This same section of code also provided a foundational legal basis for the placement of reinsurance by insurance companies (vol. II, heading XV, ch. I, art. 430). Legal conditions for reinsurance were further refined in the

Reinsurance and Coinsurance Regulations (decree no. 6/ 01 of 2 March 2001), as we shall discuss in Chapter 8.

# 3.3 FINANCIAL INSTITUTIONS LAW

All financial services in Angola, including insurance, were supposed to observe the Financial Institutions Law (*Lei de base das Instituições Financeiras*) as provided for in law no. 12/2015 of 17 June 2015. This law was intended to govern the process of establishment, conducting of business, supervision, the intervention process, and the sanctions regime for financial institutions. As defined in this law, financial institutions could be classified as either banking or non-banking (ch. I, art. 4, cl. 1). Insurance companies, reinsurance companies, and pension fund administration companies were classified as non-banking (ch. I, art. 7, cl. 2).

We shall not review all the details of this law in this case study. We would like to also stress that this was also an important piece of law for entities involved in the insurance business to ensure that they were in full compliance. As specified in this law, non-banking financial institutions should obey the rules, regulations, and laws intended for their specific activities (ch. I, art. 8, cl. 1). This meant that insurance operators should ensure that they complied with all legislation relating to insurance business. In addition, this law affirmed that ARSEG, the insurance regulatory body was responsible for regulating activities of entities involved in insurance, reinsurance, and pension funds.

## Was the Twin Peaks model of financial regulation applied in Angola?

Twin Peaks was an emerging model of financial regulation at the time of writing this book. It had been adopted in some of the leading insurance and financial markets in the world. In this model of the regulation of financial institutions, there were two distinct regulatory bodies covering the different areas of regulation as follows:
- market conduct regulatory authority
- prudential regulatory authority

We should note that the Financial Institutions Law of Angola lays the foundations for the adoption of the Twin Peaks model. Under the rubric of supervision of financial institutions, the Financial Institutions Law distinguishes concerns in respect to market conduct from issues of prudential regulation. While the legal conditions regarding market conduct were covered in articles 70 to 86 of section II, those in respect of prudential requirements were covered in articles 87 to 101 of section III. The principal idea in this approach was to allow the process of regulation of financial institutions to appropriately focus on the following principal objectives:

- Strengthen protection of consumers and ensure integrity of financial operators by looking at how the financial institutions behaved in the market. Initiatives such as Treat Customers Fairly were a key component of this approach to regulation.
- Ensure financial soundness of the operators and stability of financial markets. In order to achieve this objective, the regulatory authority focused on how financial institutions controlled risk and conditions such as capital adequacy and solvency.

One of the key aspects of Twin Peaks which had not yet been implemented in Angola in alignment with trends in key international markets was the formation of two separate regulatory bodies to cover the two distinct areas of prudential regulation and market conduct. We concluded that it would be highly beneficial for the insurance sector of Angola and of the rest of Africa if the approach of market conduct and prudential requirements were to be adopted and genuinely implemented. The market conduct conditions specified in this law, including requirements for high levels of technical competence, customer due diligence, disclosure duties, handling of complaints, code of conduct, confidentiality, conflict of interest, protection of competition, and ethical marketing (ch. VI, s. II), were all essential conditions for conducting of insurance business in alignment with one of the key traditions of insurance business: the principle of good faith. The prudential conditions regarding, amongst other conditions, capital adequacy (ch. VI, s. III, sub-s. I, art. 88) and adequate reserving (ch. VI, s. III, sub-s. I, art. 89) were critical in respect of security and financial soundness of the insurance market. We determined that an implementation in the spirit of the law in relation to the principles of good market conduct and sound prudential requirements was one of the key enabling conditions for resolution of the issue of low penetration of insurance in frontier markets, as discussed in the preface.

## Did Angola apply the anti-money-laundering and combating financing of terrorism legal framework?

As part of global efforts of the United Nations, Angola had legislation in place covering anti-money laundering and combating financing of terrorism (AML/CFT) as per law no. 34/11 of 12 December 2011. The Angolan AML/CFT legislation was in accordance with the recommended global framework. Insurance was one of the areas of focus in this legislation as part of the non-banking financial institutions referred to in this legislation (ch. I, art. 3, cl. 1b). One of the key deficiencies in the Angolan AML/CFT system was the lack of rules, regulations, and guidelines in the insurance legislation to ensure execution of all required duties, including monitoring, prevention and reporting on cases of possible money laundering and financing of terrorism.

## Were Angolan financial services subject to FATCA?

The Financial Information Tax Reporting in Compliance with the Foreign Account Tax Account Compliance Act (FATCA) was a critical pieces of legislation in respect to tax financial-information reporting requirements for financial services. It was developed in the United States and supposed to be implemented in all countries worldwide. In Angola, it was covered in presidential legislative decree (*decreto legislativo presidencial*) no. 1/17 of 20 June 2017. As per the preamble of this law, the governments of the United States and Angola agreed on 9 November 2015 that the latter would enforce compliance with the FATCA legal framework.

As specified in the legislative decree of Angola, this legal regime was part of a global initiative to combat tax evasion (*evasão fiscal*; art. 1) by improving exchange of information between tax authorities in relation to US citizens and residents with financial interests in foreign countries. The financial institutions referred to in this legal framework were supposed to provide specified reports to the local tax authorities (Administração Geral Tributária or AGT) in respect to citizens and residents of the United States holding accounts in local financial institutions. Life insurance companies and private pension funds were identified as among the financial institutions covered by this legislation (ch. I, art. 2). Table 4 outlines the categories of accounts subject to the reporting requirements in this legislation.

**Table 4: Types of Accounts Covered by the FATCA Framework**

| Category of Transaction | Types of Contracts in Insurance and Pension Business |
|---|---|
| Deposit Account | • Cash value insurance (*contratos de seguro monetizáveis*) (art. 5, cl. 3c) |
| | • Annuities (*contratos de renda*) (art. 5, cl. 3d) |
| Investment Account | • Private pension funds (art. 5, cl. 3e, item iv), excluding, inter alia, public pension funds and other public funds (art. 3) |

We have included the reporting requirements in respect of this legislation in our list of key legal reporting requirements in Appendix IV.

# 3.4 INSURANCE LAW AND REGULATIONS

Following our discussions on the aspects of the Financial Law relating to insurance, we should now discuss, in general, the legislation relating directly to insurance activities.

## Was Angola following the compliance-based or risk-based regulatory framework?

Following an analysis of emerging regulations of insurance in sub-Saharan Africa conducted by Ernst & Young, we believed that Angola had a 'simple' insurance regulatory framework at the time of writing this book. Although Angola was not specifically assessed in this study, we observed that this market matched all the key criteria of an unsophisticated regulatory framework at the bottom of the proposed rating scale (2016: 7). As we shall see in Chapter 5, the minimum capital requirements in Angola were not related to type of risks to be underwritten but based on a uniform minimum capital for all insurers. There were limited requirements for actuarial input for calculation of some of the reserves. We were of the opinion that Angola clearly had a compliance-based regulatory framework. This 'rules-based' system was the approach still followed in most African markets, as noted in the *African Insurance Regulatory Directory* (Africa Re, 2015: 41).

However, we were aware that the Angolan policymakers had started talking about plans to implement a risk-based regulatory framework, as we shall discuss later in this case study. According to Barineka Thompson (2016: 39), implementation of the risk-based approach in Africa would be in alignment with global trends and would improve 'competitiveness' of African insurers compared to international markets. If the authorities were to implement these plans and ensure appropriate enforcement; that would mark the beginning of an evolution towards a sophisticated regulatory framework. However, implementation of this new regulatory framework in Africa was likely to be achieved only in the long run due to a lack of required skills and expertise in most markets in the continent (De Leers and Chow, 2016: 49).

## What is the current insurance law of Angola?

As part of the process of market liberalization and paving the way for a shift from a closed monopoly insurance market, the policy-makers passed the General Law of Insurance Activities, as provided for in law no. 1/00 of 3 February 2000[9] (Dias, 2012: 289–309). We shall refer to this particular piece of law in this case study as the General Law of Insurance. This law was part of the current insurance legislation at the time of writing of this book.

In addition to this General Law of Insurance, there were a number of supporting pieces of legislation or regulation. We shall refer to this supporting regulatory legislation as insurance regulations. The regulations

---

[9] . Referred to in Portuguese as *Lei nº 1/00 de 3 de Fevereiro*

were intended to provide further rules and regulations to cover the different areas of insurance business. The insurance regulations include guidelines, circulars, and notices passed by the insurance regulator. We shall now discuss some of the key features of the General Law of Insurance of 2000.

# 3.5 GENERAL LAW OF INSURANCE

The General Law of Insurance consisted of fifty-three articles divided into seven chapters and two annexes. The items covered in each of the chapters of the law were as follows:

- general provisions
- control and supervision of insurance business
- insurance companies
- reinsurance and coinsurance
- insurance agency and brokerage of insurance and reinsurance
- infringements
- final and transitional provisions

Although it is not our intention in this book to discuss all the legal clauses contained in the General Law of Insurance, we shall now discuss some of the key general legal conditions covered in this piece of legislation.

## Which entities had legal capacity to do insurance business in Angola?

As stated in the General Law of Insurance, insurance business and intermediation of insurance in Angola should only be done by companies authorized by Angolan authorities in accordance with the conditions defined in this law (ch. I, art. 3, cl. 1). We should also note that the General Law of Insurance does not make specific reference to the concept of admitted insurers. Our understanding of the law is that only the insurance companies registered by the insurance regulator could be classified as admitted licenses. We shall discuss in Chapter 5 circumstances under which the regulatory authorities could permit placement abroad of risks that the local insurance market might not be willing or able to underwrite.

## Were there any barriers to entry for foreign investors in the insurance business?

We would like to begin by noting that it was crucial to address this question given that openness of the market and an enabling operating environment for business were key conditions for development of the insurance market, as identified in the Swiss Re Sigma Report on 'frontier markets' (2016: 5). In our review of the insurance legislation of Angola, we observed that there were no written legal conditions directly barring or preventing the entry of foreign investors. However, we also noted that the law places a more onerous clearance process if foreign investors have a majority stake in the business. As noted in the General Law of Insurance, a license for a new insurance company could be granted by the minister of finance unless the company had foreign investment in excess of 50 per cent. In cases where foreign investors had more than a 50 per cent share, the license had to be granted by the council of ministers (ch. I, art. 3).

Our conclusion was that the impact of the rule noted above was to make it easier to secure authorization of an insurance license where local partners had a shareholding of 50 per cent or more. Most reputable global insurance groups might not to consider as a priority investment target markets where they could not have a controlling stake in their business. In part as a consequence of this form of restriction, local shareholders tended to have a significant stake of the Angolan insurance sector, especially at the time of registration of the licenses. We noted that in some cases, key foreign investors were able to acquire more shares after registration. It appeared that there were no restrictions on foreign investors acquiring more shares at that point. From some of our experience of trying to acquire shares after an insurance company had been granted a license, the shares tended to be offered at a premium rate.

We found that one of the most important measures to minimise the risk of purely speculative investments in the insurance market was to ensure that local investors who acquired licenses demonstrated, amongst other qualities, technical competence in insurance. We were of the opinion that the insurance regulator was supposed to also verify that the new licensees would actually open offices and start operations within timeframes defined by law and that they would continue to be in full compliance with the insurance regulatory framework.

## How was competition treated in the insurance legal framework?

As specified in the General Law of Insurance, insurance companies were prohibited from any forms of restrictive practices aimed at insurance market dominance or disruption of the normal function of the market (ch. I, art. 5).The prohibition of anti-competitive practices was also provided for in the Financial Institutions Law no. 12/2015 of 17 June 2015 (art. 85, cl. 1a). As we shall discuss in Chapter 11, Angolan legislators also passed a law covering specifically the question of competition.

## What were the classes of insurance defined in the General Law of Insurance?

The classes of insurance in Angola, as stated in the General Law of Insurance (ch. I, art. 6) can be grouped in the following broad categories, as outlined in annex II of the law:
- insurance of persons
- property and pecuniary insurance
- liability insurance
- combinations of classes of insurance in the above categories

We observed that there appeared to be different structures in the grouping of classes of insurance in the law and the format used in the insurance market reports that were available at the time writing this book. The principal reporting classes of insurance in the market report were as follows (ARSEG, 2015: 105):
- life insurance
- non-life insurance
  - o accident, health, and travel
  - o fire and allied perils
  - o other property damage
  - o motor
  - o marine and aviation
  - o petrochemical
  - o liability
  - o miscellaneous

We concluded that the issue of classes of business and reporting groups could be refined in the future. It was essential to establish a consistent format in the law, market reports, and reports of the insurance market. In an area such as life insurance, for example, there should be at least a separation of life risk and savings types of business. For the non-life business, we saw a need for a more detailed categorisation of the classes of insurance business, in alignment with global standards.

## Which courts had jurisdiction over litigation involving the Angolan insurance business?

As noted in the General Law of Insurance, only Angolan courts had jurisdiction over litigation arising from the Angolan insurance business in respect to persons and entities domiciled in the national territory (ch. I, art. 8). Furthermore, the General Law of Insurance also stated that obligations arising from insurance contracts agreed upon with insurers who were not authorised in Angola were not admissible in Angolan courts, and rulings by foreign courts on such insurance contracts were not enforceable in Angola (ch. I, art. 9). However, as per the third clause of the same legal article, the law provided an exemption for cases of risks placed offshore with authorisation of the regulator, as we shall discuss further below.

## Which entity was responsible for oversight and supervision of the insurance business?

According to the General Law of Insurance, the minister of finance had the responsibility for coordination, supervision, oversight, and monitoring of the insurance business (ch. II, art. 10). The insurance regulator had authority to execute the tasks specified above (ch. II, art. 11). We should also note that at the time of passing of this law, the insurance regulator was known as Instituto de Supervisão de Seguros (ISS). As we saw in Chapter 2, this regulatory authority was replaced by a new autonomous supervisory board, ARSEG, as provided for in executive decree no. 141/13 of 27 September 2013.

## What was the official consultative organ for the insurance business?

We should note that the General Law of Insurance made provisions for an Insurance Technical Council[10] (ch. II, art. 12). Such a council was intended to function as a consultative organ under the direction of the minister of finance. It was supposed to be composed of representatives of insurance companies, private pension funds, and any other entities involved in the insurance business. The council was also supposed to analyse technical, economic, financial, and any other issues affecting the insurance business. The role and functions of this council were more fully defined in the respective regulatory framework as per the executive decree no. 66/ 2005 of 29 June 2005.

We were of the opinion that the idea of a consultative organ for the insurance sector was a good initiative, in principle. However, we believed that, in order for the organ to serve its intended purpose, it needed to have members with adequate knowledge of the insurance business. The tradition in African markets in the past was to focus more on political figures looking for prominent positions than on identifying appropriate technocrats who could make meaningful contributions. We noted that this was also one of the preoccupations raised by de Abreu (2014: 343).

## Was insurance subject to the financial disclosure regulations?

At the beginning of this chapter, we discussed the Financial Institutions Law as one of the key pieces of law which covered insurance as a non-banking financial service. We observed that part of the regulatory legislation linked to this law consisted of financial disclosure regulations as provided for in notice (*aviso*) no. 2/14 of 28 March 2014. The regulations defined the minimum requirements for information to be disclosed to the public by financial institutions in respect to their financial services and products. However, we noted that these regulations were supposed to be applicable to only the banking financial institutions as supervised by the central bank, Banco Nacional de Angola, as defined in art. 1 of the same decree.

---

[10] Referred to in Portuguese as Conselho Técnico de Seguros in the General Law of Insurance. In the regulations covering this entity, it was referred to by its name in full: Conselho Técnico de Seguros e Fundos de Pensões (CTSFP).

These disclosure regulations did not apply to non-banking financial activities, including insurance. However, we would like to point out that many of the key conditions defined in this legislation were critical for insurance business. We noted that in some of the more developed insurance markets, disclosure conditions were already part of the insurance legal framework. The main thrust of this regulation was aimed at promoting consumer protection and ensuring full disclosure of all relevant information on the products in clear, concise, and simple language. Financial institutions were also required to be fully transparent on pricing of their products and all charges, including disclosure of commissions paid to intermediaries. We hoped that these were some of the items that would be taken into account in the insurance legislation reform exercise, as we shall discuss below.

## 3.6 REFORMS OF THE INSURANCE LEGAL FRAMEWORK

At the time when we were finalising this book, we also became aware of the fact that lawmakers were planning to review and reform the insurance legal framework of Angola in the near future. The minister of finance passed decree (*despacho*) no. 87/18 of 23 March 2018,[11] which was intended to establish a task force (*grupo de trabalho*) to review the legal framework of insurance and pensions and propose reforms. As noted in the preamble of the same regulatory decree, the policymakers were of the view that the existing legislation for insurance and pensions needed to be updated in alignment with the current development of the economy. They also wanted Angola's legislation to conform to global best practices as described in the models recommended by the following entities:

- International Association of Insurance Supervisors (IAIS)
- International Organisation of Pension Supervisors (IOPS),
- Committee of Insurance, Securities, and Non-Banking Financial Authorities (CISNA), part of the initiatives of the Southern African Development Community (SADC)

---

[11] . We obtained a copy of this decree on 12/04/2018 from the website of LexLink: https://www.lexlink.eu/FileGet.aspx?FileId=3006927.

The chief executive officer (*presidente do conselho de administração*) of ARSEG, the insurance regulator, was supposed to chair the insurance reform task force consisting of identified members of the ministry of finance and the office of the regulator. The task force was supposed to be supported by a technical team from the insurance regulator's office. It was supposed to complete its work and submit a final report to the minister of finance within 270 days from 23 March 2018, the decree's date of publication. We considered this an appropriate initiative by the authorities to explore means of modernising the regulatory framework of insurance in alignment with emerging global trends. We also had the following recommendations of actions that we hoped the task force could consider:

- We had observed that there was no mention of a formal nomination of any member from other key stakeholders in the insurance sector, such as the Insurance Association, or any other representative of the other key segments in the sector, such as intermediaries and pension-fund managers. We hoped that the task force would also take note that ASAN, the Angolan insurance association, had already initiated activities aimed at proposing reforms of pieces of legislation, such as the Workmen's Compensation Act.
- Besides the regional and international organisations mentioned in the decree (IAIS, IOPS and CISNA), we believed that the task force could benefit from networking with entities such as ASEL, the insurance association for Portuguese-speaking markets (*Associação de Supervisores de Seguros Lusófonos*).
- In our view, the proposed reform of the regulatory framework was supposed to be looked at only from the point of view of legal and bureaucratic processes. We believed that there would be a need for a significant amount of technical input for a number of areas, including insurance, reinsurance, intermediation, and actuarial assistance. Given that the members of the task force consisted only of government authorities, we believed that it would be useful to find ways to secure appropriate technical assistance in this exercise.

In addition to the recommendations above, we would like to suggest that if African insurance markets wanted to attract foreign direct investments, it would be essential to aim for some form of harmonisation of regulatory frameworks. As observed in the Africa Insurance Barometer 2017, with the exception of the sixteen francophone markets in West and Central Africa, there had been no efforts to harmonise regulatory frameworks in the rest of the African markets (African Insurance Organisation, 2017: 28). It was believed that this lack harmonisation increased costs of compliance and made it harder to do business. We also believed that the insurance sector would benefit from a process of codification. As we shall see in this book, there were numerous pieces of legislation referring to insurance. There was a need in Angola to bring together all this legislation, develop appropriate support, and produce a comprehensive collection of appropriate legislation or code such as the French Code des Assurances (Vasques, 1999: 23).

# References

Achega, Gonçalo (2014), *Legislação de Mercados Financeiros, Direito Bancário e dos Seguros*. Luanda: Plural Editores.

Africa Re (2015), *The African Insurance Regulatory Directory*, analysis prepared by Dr Schanz. Zurich: Alms & Company.

African Insurance Organisation (2017), *Africa Insurance Barometer 2017*, prepared by Dr Schanz. Zurich: Alms and Company AG.

ARSEG (2015), *Desafios e Oportunidades: Estudo sobre o Sector Segurador e dos Fundos de Pensões em Angola*. Angola: PricewaterhouseCoopers Limitada.

de Abreu, Ana Edith Viegas (2014), *100 Anos de Legislação de Seguros em Angola*. Luanda - Edições Chá de Caxinde.

de Leers, Renata, and Queenie Chow (2016), 'Pricing Challenges in Africa', African Insurance Bulletin, vol. 007, May 2016.

Dias, Nélia Daniel (2012), *Legislação Financeira e dos Seguros*. Luanda: Texto Editores, Lda.

Ernst & Young (2016), *Sub-Saharan Africa: The Evolution of Insurance Regulation*. London: Ernst & Young Global Limited.

Rainha, Paula (2007), *Republic of Angola: Legal System and Research*, GlobaLex, accessed on 12/04/2018, http://www.nyulawglobal.org/globalex/Angola.html.

Swiss Re (2016), 'Insuring the Frontier Markets', *Sigma*, no. 2/2016. Zurich: Swiss Reinsurance Company Ltd.

Thompson, Barineka (2016), 'Promoting the Adoption of Risk-Based Capital in African Insurance Markets', *African Insurance Bulletin*, African Insurance Organisation, vol. no. 007, May 2016.

Vasques, José (1999), *Contrato de Seguro*, Coimbra: Coimbra Editora.

# Chapter 4

# SOCIAL INSURANCE AND PUBLIC INSURANCE FUNDS

Following our review of the insurance legal framework of Angola at the beginning of the twenty-first century, we would like to discuss the key types of obligatory insurance in the same period. In this chapter, we shall focus on the types of obligatory insurance provided by the government or public funds in this market. We shall discuss in Chapter 7 the types of obligatory insurance covered by the private insurance market. We identified eight such types of insurance or insurance-related guarantees provided by the government or public funds, as summarised in Table 5.

**Table 5: Public Insurance Mechanisms in Angola**

| YEAR | TYPE OF PUBLIC INSURANCE MECHANISMS |
|---|---|
| 2004 | National Social Security (Instituto Nacional da Segurança Social or INSS) |
|  | Insurance Guarantee Fund (Fundo de Actualização e Regularização de Seguros or FUNSEG) |
| 2005 | Fund for Actualisation of Pensions of Workmen's Accident and Occupational Illnesses (Fundo de Actualização das Pensões de Acidentes de Trabalho e Doenças Profissionais or FUNDAP) |
| 2009 | Motor Guarantee Fund (Fundo de Garantia Automóvel or FGA) |

| 2011 | Environment Impairment Fund |
| 2012 | Credit Guarantee Fund (Fundo de Garantia de Crédito) |
| 2005/16 | Aviation Insurance Guarantees for the national airline |
| 2018 | Deposit Insurance Fund (Fundo de Garantia de Depósitos) |

# 4.1 SOCIAL INSURANCE

Mehr and Cammack (1972: 379) define social insurance as a 'device for the pooling of risks by their transfer to an organisation usually governmental, that was required by law to provide pecuniary or service benefits to or on behalf of covered persons upon the occurrence of certain predesignated losses.' The principal reason social insurance schemes were set up was to prevent people from falling into 'poverty and misery' following certain unforeseen events (Naik, 2016: 3). The key features of social insurance that distinguished it from private commercial insurance were as follows (Mehr and Cammack, 1972: 379-380):

- 'Insurance cover required by law'
- 'Eligibility for benefits derived, in fact or in effect, from contributions having been made to the program by or in respect of the claimant or the person as to whom the claimant was dependent'
- 'The method for determining the benefits prescribed by law'
- 'The benefits for any individual not usually directly related to contributions made by or in respect of him/her. The benefits tended to be some form of income redistribution so as to favour certain groups such as those with low wages or a large number of dependents'
- 'The cost was borne primarily by contributions which were usually made by covered persons, their employers or both'
- 'The plan was administered or at least supervised by the government'
- 'The plan was not established by the government solely for its present or former employees'

Following our definition of social insurance, we should now look at the situation of social insurance and public insurance funds in Angola.

We were able to obtain the bulk of our references on obligatory types of insurance in Angola from the collection gathered in the book *100 Anos de Legislação de Seguros em Angola* (de Abreu, 2014: 437–489). We were also able to obtain updates of the overall legislation on the highly informative official website of Governo de Angola[12] as well as the website LexLink.[13]

## 4.2 SOCIAL SECURITY

Angola had a social security system as defined in the Social Security Basic Law no. 7/04 of 15 October of 2004 and various supporting regulations. The entity responsible for the administration of social security schemes was known as Instituto Nacional da Segurança Social (INSS). We should note that one of the major challenges faced by this fund was the lack of compliance of most employers in registering their workers and making required submissions. According to Victória da Conceição, the minister responsible for Social Welfare Family and Promotion of Women (Acção Social Família e Promoção da Mulher), the fund covered only 1.7 million workers (Novo Jornal, 2018b). This meant that more than 75 per cent of the estimated working population of 7.5 million was not covered.

**What were the levels of protection under the national social security system of Angola?**

As defined in the Social Security Basic Law, the Angolan system provided protection of basic social security (ch. II), obligatory social security (ch. III) and complementary social security (ch. IV). The key features of social security protection at these three levels were as follows:
- **Basic social security** (*protecção social de base*) was a non-contributory social grant that was supposed to be financed by taxes, public funds, donations, and any other social fundraising exercises (ch. II). It was intended to cover people exposed to extreme poverty; children with special needs or at high risk; aged people who were physically or economically dependent;

---

[12] http://www.governo.gov.ao/TodasLegislacoes.aspx
[13] https://www.lexlink.eu/legislacao/angola/legal/tudo/por-tipo-de-documentolegal

handicapped persons; and unemployed persons with a high risk of being marginalised. Assistance to appropriate target groups could be in cash or in kind.

- **Obligatory social security** (*protecção social obrigatória*) was a contributory social security insurance scheme for all working persons, whether self-employed (*por conta própria*) or employed by another party (*por conta de outrem*). The scheme was financed by contributions from employers (8 per cent) and their employees (3 per cent). The scheme covered illness, maternity, professional risk, occupational diseases, disability, age, death, and unemployment.

- **Complementary social security** (*protecção social complementar*) was a voluntary social insurance scheme subject to agreed-upon contributions from the workers and/or the employer.

The critical risk for these schemes was that the contributions were most likely to be insufficient to cover the broad range of risks that were supposed to be covered, as well as provide decent retirement pensions. We were not able to verify if the Angolan scheme had been subject to actuarial review.

We were aware that the social security regulatory framework also covered some aspects of the Workmen's Compensation Act Insurance (Nazaré, 2008: 104). As we shall see in our discussion of this type of obligatory insurance, insurers were required to submit certain reports to social security regulatory authorities. We did not observe similar requirements in the insurance regulatory framework on Mozambique. We believed that social security authorities were among the more appropriate mechanisms for handling certain aspects of WCA Insurance, such as pensions.

## 4.3 INSURANCE GUARANTEE FUND

We would like to affirm that Angola was one of few countries in Africa that created a legal framework for the setting up of an insurance guarantee fund. The main goal of the fund was to provide protection to policyholders for claims due to them in the event of insolvency of their insurer. The legal provisions for the guarantee fund in Angola were covered in decree no. 96/04 of 17 December 2004 (Achega, 2014: 498–506). This fund, known as Fundo de Actualização e Regularização de Seguros (FUNSEG), was established in the office of the insurance regulator. The regulator was supposed to direct, support, and control its operations (ch. I, art. 1). We could not obtain any financial reports on the fund, and as a result, we could not assess its financial strength.

## What was supposed to be the function of the insurance guarantee fund?

The Insurance Guarantee Fund (FUNSEG), as defined in the decree referred to above, was supposed to guarantee the reserves constituted by the insurance companies and to monitor the evaluation of assets representing the reserves setup by the insurance companies (ch. I, art. 3). General information on this entity and copies of the respective regulatory framework were available on the website of ARSEG, the insurance regulator.[14] However, as we noted above, we were not able to locate any financial reports on the performance of this fund. We believed that it would be important for this fund to improve levels of transparency as to their financial situation. It was also important for the fund to report on cases where the interests of policyholders would have benefited from its protection.

## 4.4 PUBLIC FUND FOR PENSIONS OF WORK ACCIDENTS

We noted that work-related accidents were supposed to be covered by a combination of a private insurance policy as well as a public fund in respect of the pension claims, as provided for in the Workmen's Compensation Act Insurance Legal Framework, contained in decree no. 53/05 of 5 August 2005. We shall discuss the obligatory insurance provided by the commercial insurance market in the next chapter. For now, we would like to briefly review the public fund in respect to this obligatory form of insurance.

---

[14] http://www.arseg.ao/index.php?option=com_content&view=article&id=127 &Itemid=180&lang=pt (accessed on 01 July 2018)

## What was supposed to be the function of the public WCA pension funds?

As stated in the Workmen's Compensation Act insurance legal framework, a Fund for Actualisation of Pensions of Workmen's Accident and Occupational Illnesses (Fundo de Actualização das Pensões de Acidentes de Trabalho e Doenças Profissionais or FUNDAP) was supposed to be set up by the minister of finance (ch. VIII, art. 42). We supported this approach of the Angolan authorities in considering mechanisms to protect pension funds arising from WCA insurance claims. We also made recommendations for similar measures to address the same type of issue in the WCA insurance regulatory framework of Mozambique, as discussed in *Development of Insurance in Mozambique* (2017: 293). We believed that in the event of failure of an insurance company, it was vital to ensure that the long-term reserves in respect to these pensions were appropriately protected.

Furthermore, we noted that from the early days of development of WCA insurance in Europe, it tended to be treated as part of social insurance (Nazaré, 2008: 76). In most African insurance markets, WCA insurance was handled as part of the business of private-sector insurance markets. Although in Angola, WCA insurance was also underwritten as part of private insurance, it was partly subject to the social security regulatory framework, and some aspects of its claims were covered by the public pensions fund, as noted above.

## 4.5 MOTOR GUARANTEE FUND

As we shall discuss in Chapter 7, motor third-party liability was supposed to be an obligatory form of insurance. Notwithstanding the existence of this legal requirement, we found that not all road-users complied with the law. In addition, there was a risk that the policy could be invalid or ineffective. It was possible that the insured motorist could fail to satisfy all the conditions of the respective policy, making it possible for the insurer to reject the claim or cancel the policy. It was for this purpose that it was deemed necessary to set up a mechanism to protect innocent third-party victims of road accidents through what was known as a Motor Guarantee Fund (Fundo de Garantia Automóvel or FGA). The fund in Angola followed a model similar to that of Portugal, as presented on the website of ASF,[15] the Portuguese insurance regulator.

## How was the Motor Guarantee Fund of Angola supposed to function?

The setting up of the FGA in Angola was provided for in decree no. 10/09 of 13 July 2009 (Dias, 2012: 389–403). The fund was intended to cover liability in the event of accidents involving third parties without the obligatory motor third-party liability or in the event of a hit-and-run accident (AXCO, 2011: 3). According to the statutes of the FGA, it was supposed to cover accidents involving invalid or ineffective motor third-party liability policies or situations where the involved insurer would be declared insolvent (ch. I, art. 2, cl. 2).

We found that the website of the insurance regulators contained general background information on the FGA.[16] However, we were not able to locate other key information, such as annual financial accounts of the fund. We believed that it was crucial for such public institutions to be transparent about their activities, like the good example we identified in Chapter 1 when we discussed the performance of BODIVA, the new Angolan stock exchange. We also noted a news item in *Jornal de Angola* questioning whether this fund was even functional, although it was collecting required contributions (Silva, 2018).

Notwithstanding the complaints about lack of indications that the fund was paying any claims, we would like to point out that there could be a larger problem than simple reluctance to settle claims of third parties. As we observed at the beginning of this book, Angola had one of the lowest rates of penetration of insurance. If most people did not insure their vehicles due to a lack of awareness of the essence of insurance, there would possibly be a high frequency of accidents involving uninsured vehicles. The

---

[15]  http://www.asf.com.pt/NR/exeres/79F6CDBB-EEFB-4637-9378-E13D350 DEF69.htm

[16]  Information on FGA found on the ARSEG website at http://www.arseg.ao/index. php?option=com_content&view=article&id=137&Itemid=175&lang=pt (accessed 16/05/2018).

fund could also be easily overwhelmed by many uninsured claims, and this would make the concept financially unsustainable.

According to the statutes of the fund, it was supposed to be financed by, amongst other sources, a levy of 5 per cent of premiums of all motor business generated by the private insurance market (ch. II, art. 8). This levy was supposed to be an additional charge applied on the net premium for all types of business, including own damage. We should note that like the fund in Portugal, the Angolan fund had the right to recover (*direito de regresso*) from the vehicle responsible for the accident after assuming subrogation (*sub-rogação*) rights from the third party affected by the accident (ch. I, art. 7).

Finally, we would like to note that in addition the legislation involving formation of the FGA, there was also a ministerial decree no. 9/03 of 21 February 2003[17] which provided regulations regarding the calculation and setting up of the solvency margin (*margem de solvência*) of the fund. This was a vital process to monitor and ensure financial soundness of the fund. However, we could not locate any reports on the financial performance of the fund in order to ascertain if it was solvent or could be facing challenges. If there were far more uninsured vehicles than insured ones as a result of the persistent problem of low penetration of insurance, there would be more claims than available funds. This would be directly reflected in, amongst other things, the solvency margins of the fund. In the case of deterioration of the solvency margin, the fund would probably have to rely on a bail-out from the national government.

## 4.6 ENVIRONMENTAL IMPAIRMENT FUND

We also noted that there was a reference to some form of public fund in presidential decree no. 194/11 of 7 July 2011 in respect to liability for environmental damages (*responsabilidade por danos ambientais*). We shall briefly discuss how this fund was supposed to operate.

---

[17] Referred to in Portuguese as *despacho no. 9/03 de 21 de Fevereiro.*

## How was the environmental impairment fund supposed to operate?

As stated in the regulations referred to above, there was supposed to be a contribution of 1 per cent to a public fund for the cost of prevention and for repair of the environment. The public fund was supposed to intervene in cases where the polluter was unknown or did not have financial resources or other means to provide redress (ch. IV, art. 23). We also noted reference to this environmental impairment fund in the mining code (part I, vol. IV, ch. XVI, s. II, sub-s. V, art. 267). It was stated in this law that contributions were required to be made to this fund from all mining activities, except for small-scale mines.

We could not trace any other piece of legislation referring to the formal establishment of this fund with regulations on how it was supposed to operate. This was a critical issue, given the significant scale of extractive industries—especially mining, oil, and gas—in Angola. We also noted that presidential decree no. 194/11 of 7 July 2011 and the mining code also referred to other obligatory guarantees and insurance policies that were supposed to be obtained from the private financial markets. We shall discuss these in Chapter 7 as part of the unregulated compulsory forms of covers.

# 4.7 CREDIT GUARANTEE FUND

## Was there a credit guarantee fund in Angola?

Although the regulations for the setting up of a credit guarantee fund (*fundo de garantia de crédito*) were passed in 2012, the scheme appeared not to have become operational by the time of writing this book. The fund was supposed to have been established in accordance with presidential decree (*decreto presidencial*) no. 78/12 of 4 May 2012. We believed that this was an important aspect for further review by Angolan policymakers. Instead of trying to create a new public fund for credit guarantees, one of the options that could be considered was for Angola to join the African Trade Insurance Agency (ATI).[18] This agency already provided trade credit insurance and related types of insurance for other African member-states.

---

[18] Information on ATI can be found on its website at http://www.ati-aca.org/ (accessed on 15/06/2018).

# 4.8 DEPOSIT INSURANCE SCHEME

## Did Angola have deposit insurance?

The Deposit Insurance Fund (DIF) and Deposit Guarantee Fund (DGF) were among the key contemporary mechanisms for protecting the financial interests of private citizens in the event of failure of financial institutions where they might have their earnings and savings deposited. The Financial Institutions Law specified that policymakers had the responsibility to set up this form of mechanism to protect funds of private citizens (ch. VI, s. I, art. 69). Notwithstanding this recognition of the importance of deposit insurance in the current regulatory framework, Angola did not have such a form of protection of bank deposits up to the first half of 2018.

According to a paper on deposit protection schemes by Demirgüç-Kunt et al (2005: 2), there would always be some form of 'implied deposit insurance scheme'. This was due to the fact that in the event of occurrence of major 'systemic banking distress', the government would be under high political pressure to provide some form of relief or bail-out. However, as we were preparing to publish this book, the Angolan regulatory authorities passed presidential decree no. 195/ 18 of 22 August 2018, which was intended to pave the way for the creation of a DGF in Angola. Since this fund had not yet started operating, we could not comment on its performance. However, we shall see if in the future, it will actually be set up and if it will operate as expected.

# 4.9 OTHER FORMS OF GOVERNMENT GUARANTEES

We found the following two cases where the Angolan government assumed legal liability in respect of insurance of public entities:

1. According to a joint executive decree by the ministries of finance and transport (no. 52/05 of 9 May 2005), the Angolan state made an exceptional assumption of aviation war and terrorism risks for TAAG, the national airline. The government had assumed risk up to US$1 billion in excess of a US$50 million limit of liability imposed by the international insurance market.

2. According to resolution no. 115/09 of 18 December 2009,[19] the Council of Ministers determined that the Angolan state would temporarily assume part of the liability arising from the fleet of TAAG for aviation hull, aviation spares, and aviation liability sections in excess of the net retention of the national insurer ENSA. This measure was intended to protect the retention of ENSA during the period that TAAG flights to the European Union were blacklisted from 2007 to 2009 due to concerns regarding standards of civil aviation safety (Macauhub, 2009). The blacklisting resulted in extraordinary accumulation of liability for ENSA following withdrawal of international reinsurance capacity. The ban was partially lifted in 2009 and was only fully removed in 2016 (Correia, 2016 and Macauhub, 2016).

Besides the two pieces of legislation referred to above, we could not locate any other information on how this exposure was handled by the state. It appeared to us that the measures that were implemented could be viewed as some form of self-insurance. We did not know how this assumed or retained risk was planned and funded, since we did not find any other public facility used to handle such risks and how the government could ensure financial solvency of the respective facility.

In this chapter, we looked at different forms of public insurance capacity. First, we looked at the social security fund as a clear case of a public insurance fund that was already in place. Second, we discussed the case of the recently established fund for protection of bank deposits. Third, we reviewed cases of funds that appeared to be in the process of being set up for credit guarantee and motor guarantee. Fourth, we looked at the situation where the national government had to provide some forms of aviation insurance guarantees to the national insurer for shortfall of cover for the national airline. In the next chapter, we shall start to look at the conditions for setting up and running an insurance company in the private insurance market.

---

[19] Denoted in Portuguese as *'Resolução no. 115/09 de 18 de Dezembro'*

# References

Achega, Gonçalo (2014), *Legislação de Mercados Financeiros, Direito Bancário e dos Seguros*. Luanda: Plural Editores.

AXCO (2011), *Angola: Non-Life Insurance Market Report*, London: AXCO Insurance Information Services.

Correia, Raquel Almeida (2016), '*Ao fim de nove anos, a angolana TAAG volta a sobrevoar a Europa*', in *Público*, https://www.publico. pt/2016/06/10/economia/noticia/ao-fim-nove-anos-a-angolana-taag-volta-a-sobrevoar-o-ceu-da-europa-1734748 (accessed 20 May 2018).

de Abreu, Ana Edith Viegas (2014), *100 Anos de Legislação de Seguros em Angola*. Luanda: Edições Chá de Caxinde.

Demirgüç-Kunt, Asli, Baybars Karacaovali, and Luc Laeven (2005), 'Deposit Insurance around the World: A Comprehensive Database', on the World Bank website http://siteresources. worldbank.org/INTRES/Resources/469232-1107449512766/ DepositInsuranceDatabasePaper_DKL.pdf (accessed 16/04/2018).

Dias, Nélia Daniel (2012), *Legislação Financeira e dos Seguros*, Luanda: Texto Editores, Lda.

Macauhub (2009), 'Angola: TAAG Prepares for Evaluation and Hopes to Re-launch Flights to Europe in July', https://macauhub.com. mo/2009/03/05/6664/ (accessed 20 May 2018).

Macauhub (2016), 'Angolan Airline TAAG Removed from EU Blacklist', 14 June 2016, https://macauhub.com.mo/2016/06/14/angolan-airline-taag-removed-from-eu-blacklist/ (accessed 20 May 2018).

Mehr, Robert I., and Cammack, Emerson (1972), Principles of Insurance. Illinois: Richard D. Irwin, Inc.

Muchena, Israel (2018), *Development of Insurance in Mozambique*. Bloomington: AuthorHouse.

Naik, Dhirendra Narayan (2016), 'Social Security and Social Insurance', in *Journal of Civil and Legal Sciences*, vol. 5, no. 5, https://www.omicsonline.org/open-access/social-security-and-social-insurance-2169-0170-1000206.pdf (accessed 28 May 2018).

Nazaré, Domingas Miguel (2008), *A ENSA e a Reforma do Sector Seguradora em Angola*, Luanda–Caxinde: Editora e Livraria.

Novo Jornal (2018), 'Seguranca Social: Apenas 1,7 dos 7,5 Milhões de Trabalhadores Estão Inscritos', http://www.novojornal.co.ao/sociedade/interior/seguranca-social-apenas-17-dos-75-milhoes-de-trabalhadores-estao-inscritos-57493.html?utm_term=Bom+dia%2C+sim.+-+Newsletter+Novo+Jornal&utm_campaign=Newsletters&utm_source=e-goi&utm_medium=email (accessed 26 August 2018).

Silva, Victor (2018), 'Fundo de Garantia Automóvel Angolano é um Fiasco', *Jornal de Angola*, http://jornaldeangola.sapo.ao/opiniao/fundo_de_garantia_automovel__angolano_e_um_fiasco (accessed 18 May 2018).

Chapter 5

# INSURANCE COMPANIES

*Everyone can learn to deal with risk and uncertainty.*
*Everyone who dares to know.*

*—Gerd Gigerenzer at TEDxZurich*

Following our discussions on social and public insurance in the last chapter, we now look at the key conditions for setting up and doing insurance business in the private insurance market in Angola. We shall discuss the status and types of entities that were permitted to do insurance business in Angola and how the companies were supposed to be set up. For the purpose of this review, we shall focus on the rules and regulations as defined in the General Law of Insurance and executive decree no. 5/03 of 24 January 2003, containing the regulations on conditions of access and conduct of business of insurers.

Furthermore, we should note the following other key pieces of regulations, circulars, and directives in respect of operations of insurance companies:

- Decree no. 7/02 of 9 April 2002: Transgressions of Insurance Legislation and Sanctions Regime
- Decree no. 79-A/02 of 5 December 2002: Chart of Accounts for Insurance Companies
- Executive decree no. 58/02 of 5 December 2002: Guidelines on Insurance Rating Systems, which we shall simply refer to in this book as *rating guidelines*

- Executive decree no. 6/03 of 24 January 2003: Regulations on Financial Guarantees
- Decree no, 9/03 of 21 February 2003: Regulations on the Calculation of the Solvency Margin and Setting up of a Guarantee Fund.
- Decree no. 53/05 of 15 August 2005: Legal Framework of Insurance of Workmen's Compensation and Occupational Illnesses
- Executive decree no. 66/05 of 29 June 2005: Regulations of the Insurance and Pensions Technical Council
- Executive decree no. 70/06 of 7 June 2006: Revision of Minimum Capital Requirements for Insurance Companies.
- Executive decree no. 74/07 of 29 June 2007: Regulations to Streamline the Current Conditions for Accessing and Operating in the Insurance Market
- Circular no. 01/ISS/MF/10 of 2 March 2010: Directive on Rejected Motor Third Party Liability Insurance
- Circular no. 02/ISS/MF/10 of 1 July 2010: Directive on Required Formats of Obligatory Periodical Reports from Insurance Companies to the Insurance Regulator.
- Circular no. 05/ISS/MF/10 on 2 August 2010: Guarantees in Favour of the Insurance Public Guarantee Fund
- Circular no. 06/ISS.MF/10 of 2 August 2010 on insurance intermediation
- Circular no. 01/FGA/MF/10: Reporting model to be followed in the quarterly submissions to the Motor Guarantee Fund
- Circular no. 30/GAPCAARSEG/14 of 5 August 2014: Directive on Submissions of Reports of Suspicious Operations and Identification of Designated Persons
- Notice no. 2/15 of 29 December 2015: Regulations in respect of execution of obligations of identification and due diligence as well as establishment of a programme of action on anti-money-laundering and combating of financing of terrorism
- Executive decree no. 464/16 of 1 December 2016: Update of Fines in Respect of Infringement of the Insurance Law

# 5.1 REGISTRATION AND ESTABLISHMENT OF AN INSURANCE COMPANY

## What were the key conditions and criteria for authorisation of an insurance license?

Requests for an insurance license were subject to evaluation by the insurance regulator using the following requirements and criteria, as defined in the General Law of Insurance (ch. III, s. II, sub-s. I, art. 14):

- quality of services to be provided to the public
- fitness, propriety, and solvency of the founding shareholders
- efficiency of technical and financial resources as per the respective feasibility study
- compatibility between prospects of development of the insurance company and maintenance of healthy competition in the market

In addition to the above, as specified in the second clause of article 14, the granting of a new insurance license was also based on the criteria of opportunities and needs arising from the economic and financial situation of the country and in relation to the specific interests of the insurance market.

Furthermore, as stated in the General Law of Insurance, a business feasibility study was supposed to be submitted with the application (ch. III, s. II, sub-s. I, art. 15). The required study was supposed to contain financial projections for at least the first three years of business operations as well as a financial analysis. The financial analysis would take into account the rules regarding financial guarantees and reinsurance as defined in the regulations of the insurance legal framework, as discussed below. We should note that all documents for application of a new license were supposed be translated into Portuguese and authenticated (ch. VII, art. 49).

Finally, we would like to point out that although the key conditions for registering an insurance or a reinsurance company appeared to be clear and straightforward, the actual process could take many years due to a number of critical conditions and considerations not defined in the legislation. As we shall discuss in Chapter 8, there was the case involving the licensing of the national reinsurer that remained pending following the approval of the articles of incorporation of the same company nearly two decades earlier.

## What information was to be submitted with an application for a new insurance company license?

The documents that were supposed to be submitted in the application for a new license, as provided for in the Regulations on Conditions of Access and Conduct of Business of Insurers (ch. I, art. 1), included the following:

- detailed presentation of reasons justifying the setting up of the company
- indication of the corporate name (*denominação social*), draft company statutes, and organogramme
- indication of the general insurance-policy conditions and technical basis of underwriting for the classes of insurance to be covered as well as the company's approach to reinsurance
- declaration of commitment that at the time of setting up of the company, the minimum capital required would be raised
- identification of the founding shareholders and their respective shareholding
- police clearance certificates issued in a period of less than ninety days for the individual founding shareholders as well as for the directors and managers, in the case of shareholding by a corporate entity
- declaration testifying that the individual founding shareholders as well as directors and managers representing corporate investors had never been declared insolvent or bankrupt
- presentation of the balance sheets for the last three years for the three potential principal shareholders and a report on the current financial status in the case of application by a corporate entity
- board resolution conferring authority to the members of the board of directors. The board of directors and all other corporate governance bodies were required to include representation of Angolan citizens.

## Which governing bodies were required by law in an insurance company?

From our review of the commercial law and the Regulations on Conditions of Access and Conduct of Business of Insurers, we noted the following principal governing bodies (*orgãos sociais*) required by law:

- board of the general assembly (*mesa da assembleia geral*)
- board of directors (*conselho de administração*)
- audit committee (*conselho fiscal*)
- external auditor (*auditor externo*)

We also observed from the published accounts of one of the major Angolan insurers, NOSSA Seguros, that they had set up other internal control bodies, including a committee for risk management policy (*política de gestão de risco*). They found it necessary to implement this measure in order to align with their principal shareholder, a banking institution (NOSSA, 2017: 8). As defined in the Financial Institutions Law, financial institutions should have efficient processes for identification, management, control, and reporting on risks to which the institution could be exposed (ch. II, s. I, art. 15, item g). We were also aware that the same risk management processes would be a critical element of the emerging risk-based insurance regulatory framework. The Angolan regulatory authorities were considering this new regulatory approach as part of planned future reform exercises.

## How long would it take to register a new insurance company?

According to the Regulations on Conditions of Access and Conduct of Business of Insurers, subject to satisfactory submission of a complete application with all the required documents, the insurance regulator should complete review of new applications within ninety days and deliver to the minister of finance for final approval (ch. I, art. 2, cl. 1). However, the minister of finance could extend this period up to an undefined number of days (ch. I, art. 2, cl. 2). The insurance regulator could request additional clarifications or items and carry out verifications deemed necessary, notwithstanding the period noted above.

Furthermore, the same regulations were not intended to apply any pressure on the authorities to be accountable and to provide feedback to prospective investors. The regulations clearly specified that if there were no communications from the authorities within the defined period, the investors would view this as an implied rejection and not see such a situation as amounting to an acceptance (ch. I, art. 2, cl. 3). From our experience of trying to register an insurance company in Angola, the registration process described above was one of the major bottlenecks, especially for foreign insurers intending to set up in this market.

## What legal forms of entities could be established as insurers?

According to the General Law of Insurance, an insurance company could be in the form of three types of legal entities (ch. III, s. I, art. 13). First, it could be in the form of a public limited liability company with investments of public funds, private investors, or a combination of public and private shareholders. Second, they could also be in the form of mutual insurers (*mútuas de seguros*) or cooperative insurance companies or similar types of organization provided that they were established with the corporate objective of underwriting of insurance business. Third, an insurer or reinsurer could be in the form of an agency of an international insurance or reinsurance company for which Angola was a shareholding member-state. Such an agency would require specific authorisation by the insurance regulator.

At the time of researching this case study, all the insurers operating in Angola were in the form of public limited companies. The oldest two insurers, ENSA and AAA Seguros, had public shareholding. The rest were owned predominantly by private shareholders. There were no mutual insurance companies or cooperatives or insurance agencies authorised to do business in Angola. There were also no entities operating as local branch offices of insurers incorporated abroad. All the insurers had been appropriately incorporated with their head offices and registered offices in Angola

## On what basis could an insurance license be withdrawn?

According to the General Law of Insurance of 3 February 2000 (ch. III, s. II, sub-s. I, art. 16), an insurance license could be withdrawn under the following circumstances:

- It was found that the license had been obtained on the basis of false declarations.
- The insurance company ceased to operate or significantly reduced business for a period of more than six months.
- The insurer failed to comply with any of the legal conditions for doing business as required by the law.

We should note that at the time of researching this case study, we could not trace any formal notifications of withdrawal of any insurance license. However, we were aware that a number of insurance licenses were either dormant or inactive. Some of the registered insurers had not initiated operations since their registration. We were also aware of reports from some market observers that AAA Seguros had suspended operations completely (AXCO: 2018: 3). We should note that this weakness of the regulatory framework as well as a lack of consistency and poor enforcement were not unique to Angola. The same key issues could be found in many other African insurance markets, as was reported in the *Africa Insurance Barometer 2017* (AIO, 2017: 28).

## On what basis could authorization of an insurer expire?

As stated in the General Law of Insurance, authorisation of an insurance license could expire if the entities applying for a license expressly withdrew their application or if the insurance company was not set up within six months after granting of its license (ch. III, s. II, sub-s. I, art. 17). As stipulated in the same section of insurance law, in cases that were appropriately justified, the minister of finance could extend the period of validity of the license by a further ninety days. At the time of doing our research for the publication of this book, we were not aware of any formal confirmation of expiration of any of the licenses of the authorised insurance companies.

## Where should insurance companies be registered?

According to the General Law of Insurance, insurers were required to make a special registration with the insurance regulator before commencing any business activities (ch. III, s. II, sub-s. II, art. 18). As noted above, the insurance regulatory authority at the time of writing of this book was ARSEG. As specified in the same piece of legislation, after the formal setting up of an insurance company, it was supposed to begin operations within a period of six months (ch. III, s. II, sub-s. III, art. 20). We have already discussed above the process of expiration that could occur if the insurer failed to initiate business within this time frame.

## What were the rules regarding foreign investment in the insurance business?

In addition to the standard rules and criteria for application for a new insurance license as discussed above, there were additional requirements for foreign investors specified in the General Law of Insurance (ch. III, s. III, art. 22), as follows:

- At least 60 per cent of the foreign investment capital should be from insurance and financial institutions.
- At least 30 per cent of the subscribed, raised, and/or authorised capital should be from Angolan entities, which could be any of the following:
  o private business
  o public entity
  o mixed private/public entities
  o collective persons or individuals
  o public funds that generated their own revenue and were not dependent on state budget
- Foreign investors should obtain from an appropriate authority in their country a certificate of good standing in insurance business.
- The foreign investing business entities should provide their business statutes.

We should point out that with the passage of the new Private Investments Law no. 10/18 of 26 June 2018, policy-makers removed conditions stipulating a minimum requirement for local shareholding. In the planned reform of the insurance regulatory framework, we felt that the policy-makers could try to align the conditions of the insurance legislation with the Private Investments Law.

# 5.2 FINANCIAL REQUIREMENTS FOR AN INSURER

## What were the minimum capital requirements for an insurance license?

As stated in the General Law of Insurance, insurance companies were supposed to maintain the statutory minimum amounts of capital stipulated in the current insurance regulatory framework (ch. III, s. IV, sub-s. I, art. 23). At the time of writing this book, the most recent minimum capital requirements for the different types of insurance business as specified in executive Decree no. 70/06 of 7 June 2006 (art. 1) were as follows:

- US$10 million for a composite license
- US$8 million for a life Insurance business
- US$6 million for a non-life business

We should note that all the registered insurance companies at the time of writing this book had composite licenses. We had also observed that there were no specific provisions for appropriate capital requirements regarding microinsurance. We were also not aware of any licensed insurer that was exploring microinsurance. It appeared that the oil and gas insurance business was the principal goal of most of the registered companies. We also noted in these regulations revising the minimum capital requirements, there was no reference to the new capital requirements for mutual insurers. The minimum capital for mutual insurers as defined in the prior regulations of 2003[20] had been set at US$200,000 (ch. II, art. 5).

---

[20] These regulations were provided for in executive decree no. 5/03 of 24 January 2003.

## What reserves were to be maintained by an insurer?

As stated in the General Law of Insurance, insurance companies operating in the Angolan insurance market were required to maintain a legal reserve as well as statutory technical reserves and any other additional provisions deemed appropriate (ch. III, s. IV, sub-s. I). We shall not discuss all the rules and regulations in respect of how these reserves were supposed to be constituted and maintained. The types of reserves that were required as defined in the insurance legal framework of Angola were as follows:

- There was a requirement for a legal reserve (*reserva legal*) of 10 per cent of annual net profits up to 50 per cent of the share capital, as defined in the Regulations on Conditions of Access and Conduct of Business of Insurers. (ch. III, art. 8)
- Unexpired risk reserves (*provisões para riscos em curso*) were required for all classes of insurance business except for life and WCA insurance reserves that were supposed to be subject to actuarial review. We noted in the Regulations on Financial Guarantees that insurers were supposed to calculate the unexpired risk reserves on a contract-by-contract and pro rata basis (ch. I, art.1, cl. 2). However, as an option provided in the same regulations, an insurer could calculate this reserve on a global basis, subject to authorization by the insurance regulator (ch. I, art.1, cl. 3). The regulations also provided a guideline of rates that could be applied for this global basis as follows:
  - o 33.33 per cent of gross written premium for classes of business where the majority of contracts had a cover period of one year
  - o 10 per cent of gross written premium for classes of business where the majority of the contracts had a cover period of less than one year
- Actuarial reserves (*provisões matemáticas*) were required for life insurance
- There was a requirement for actuarial reserves for Workman's Compensation Act (WCA) insurance
- Reserves for temporary disability (*provisões para incapacidades temporárias*) were also required for WCA insurance. As provided for in the regulations on financial guarantees, this reserve should

be calculated at 25 per cent of the gross written premium net of reversals and cancellations

- The regulations stipulated outstanding losses reserves (*provisões para sinistros pendentes*), which were supposed to be calculated on a claim-by-claim basis as per the guideline provided in the financial guarantees regulations (ch. I, art. 5). In the same regulations, it was stated that in the event of an abnormally large claim, the insurance regulator could authorise the concerned insurer to only make provisions and provide financial guarantees for the value which corresponded to the retention of the insurer net of reinsurance (ch. II, art. 8). This was a vital condition, given that there could be huge losses for risks such as those of the oil and gas sector, which would tend to be heavily reinsured. The global reinsurers covering such types of risks tended not to be keen to deposit premium and loss reserves for most territories. They had concerns about being exposed to foreign currency risk and impairment of their financial interest as a result of poor sovereign rating in domicile of risk. We shall discuss later in this chapter the mechanisms that were in place to provide guarantees for the reserves retained locally in Angola.

- Equalisation reserves (*provisões para desvios de sinistralidade*) were required for classes of business that by their nature could have exceptionally high loss ratio, such as credit insurance, as specified in the financial guarantees regulations (ch. I, art. 6). There was an exemption from setting up of this reserve for insurers where this type of risk represented less than 4 per cent of their insurance business portfolio. We were not aware of any insurer that was underwriting credit insurance.

In addition to the reserves required by law as noted above, insurance companies could set up other free reserves (*reservas livres*) provided that they informed the insurance regulator before this was done, as stated in the Regulations on Conditions of Access and Conduct of Business of Insurers (ch. III, art. 9). In the following article in the same regulatory legislation, it was noted that insurers could not distribute any amounts of money as dividends or any form of security which reduced in any manner the legal reserve fund below minimum required levels.

## What were the set limits for investments in insurance companies?

According to the General Insurance Law, the assets representing the financial reserves constituted by the insurer were supposed be in compliance with the structure and criteria defined in the regulatory framework (ch. III, s. IV, sub-s. II, art. 31). The limits of the financial investment of the reserves were as defined in the Regulations on Conditions of Access and Conduct of Business of Insurers (ch. IV, s. I, art.11-12), as summarised in Table 6.

**Table 6: Investment Limits for Insurance Companies**

| Type of Investment | | Life Insurance | Non-Life Insurance |
|---|---|---|---|
| a) | Government Bonds (*títulos do estado*) | 22% to 70% | 23.5% to 80% |
| b) | Bonds (*obrigações*), equity securities (*títulos de participação*), or other negotiable debt securities (*títulos negociávewas de dívida*), including cash bonds (*obrigações de caixa*) | 19% to 60% | 23.5% to 80% |
| c) | Shares of joint-stock companies (*acções de sociedades anónimas*) | 16% to 50% | 14.5% to 50% |
| d) | Investment in venture capital funds (*fundos de capital de risco*) | 12.5% to 40% | 11.5% to 40% |
| e) | Unit-linked investment funds (*unidades de participação em fundos de investimento*) | 9% to 30% | 9% to 30% |
| f) | Mortgage loans (*empréstimos hipotecários*) and non-industrial buildings | 12.5% to 40% | 9% to 30% |
| g) | Cash, deposits in credit institutions, and investment in interbank money market | 9% to 30% | 9% to 30% |

In addition to the limits of investment portfolios as noted above, the **Regulations on Conditions of Access and Conduct of Business of Insurers** also provided guidelines aimed at attainment of prudential diversification of investment (Ch. IV, s. II, art.13). The limits were intended to mitigate the concentration of investment in any one interest. For more details on the applicable guidelines please review these regulations.

## Were local insurers permitted to invest abroad?

According to the rules and regulations defined in the Regulations on Conditions of Access and Conduct of Business of Insurers, a life insurer could apply to the minister of finance for authorisation to invest in shares and bonds quoted on foreign stock exchanges that were duly regulated and functioning properly (ch. IV, s. I, art. 11, cl. 2). If approved, the limits that would be applicable for such investments would be as per items b), c) and d) in Table 6. We noted that this was an important concession, given that there was no stock exchange in Angola at the time of passing of this legislation. Up to 2015, Angola remained one of few countries in southern Africa without a stock exchange despite the growing significance of its economy. However, a new debt and stock exchange, known as BODIVA[21] SGMR[22] (BODIVA, 2015: 3), launched in 2015. Given that available options on BODIVA were limited to public debt securities (Angop, 2017), investors in the Angola market still needed access to foreign markets. Therefore, it was vital for the concession to invest in foreign stock exchange as noted above to be maintained.

## What were the solvency requirements?

In addition to the financial reserves referred to above, the General Law of Insurance stipulated that insurers were required to comply with the solvency regulatory framework (ch. III, s. IV, sub-s. II, art. 32). The framework was intended to ensure that the insurance companies would be able to fulfil their obligations in the long term. The methodology for calculating of the solvency margins in Angola was covered in the Financial Guarantees Regulations (ch. III). The minimum required solvency margins were as follows:

- 14 per cent of minimum required capital for companies underwriting both life and non-life business
- 12 per cent of minimum required capital for companies underwriting only non-life business
- 16 per cent of minimum required capital for companies underwriting only life business

---

[21] Acronym for *Bolsa de Dívida e Valores de Angola*

[22] Abbreviation for *Sociedade Gestora de Mercados Regulamentados*, which could be translated to English as Management Company of Regulated Markets

The solvency margins were supposed to be calculated in alignment with the formula defined in the same regulatory framework. The required margins were the same for all companies regardless of the fact that the underwriters could be planning to underwrite different types of risks. These were some of the areas we believed needed to be addressed in the planned review of the regulatory framework.

## Was there solvency relief for reinsured portion of risk?

The solvency regulatory model of Angola did not provide relief for the portion of risk placed through proportional reinsurance. The basis for calculating the liability of the insurer as defined in annex no. 7 of the Financial Guarantees Executive Decree no. 6/03 of 24 January 2003 was based on gross premium income of the insurer, including ceded reinsurance. This would create a situation where insurers needed to transfer a significant portion of the written premium to reinsurers for the reinsurance requirements of their business whilst at the same time needing to maintain locally sufficient financial assets to cover their gross liability, including reinsured portion of risk, as required in the statutory solvency requirements (ch. III, art. 15).

This lack of relief for the reinsured portion of risks in the calculation of the liability of the insurer for the purposes of verification of adequacy of solvency levels would affect the capital requirements of the insurer. At the same time, it would not be prudent for insurers to avoid reinsurance placement of exposure in excess of their capacity. Reinsurance was required to ensure financial soundness of the insurer by maintaining retention of risk within its financial capacity or by avoiding risks where there might be limited scope for spread of risk. The oil and gas sector of Angola was one such area, with massive values at risk that were far beyond the financial capacity of the local insurance market.

# 5.3 REPORTING REQUIREMENTS

## What were the key insurance-related obligatory reporting requirements for insurers in Angola?

The insurance regulator issued a guideline covering a handful of the principal reporting requirements as per circular no. 02/ISS/MF/10 of 1 July 2010. From our review of the different pieces of legislation within the current Insurance Legal Framework, we identified fifty-one obligatory reporting requirements for insurance companies, as outlined in appendix IV. We did not include on this list the reporting requirements regarding tax, labour, national statistics, and other legal requirements for business entities. We focused only on requirements from the insurance regulatory framework as well as key financial legislation affecting insurance.

We were of the view that the regulator needed to update the official guideline, since many of the actual obligatory reports were not specified. We also observed that some reporting requirements were unclear. For instance, regarding submissions of annual accounts, the main insurance law stipulated a timeline of 31 March (ch. III, s. II, sub-s. IV, art. 37, cl. 1), while the circular from the regulator specified 30 April (ch. II, art. 2). We considered the period specified in the circular to be more realistic. However, it was crucial to ensure that there were no contradictions in the regulatory framework.

We also believed that it would be useful to provide all the identified reporting requirements in appropriate places, such as the website of the regulatory body. We saw the case of the list of reporting requirements[23] as provided on the website of ASF,[24] the insurance regulator in Portugal. We have presented our list in Appendix IV. We also believed that it would be beneficial for the insurance market to rationalize reporting requirements. We were of the opinion that it would be better to have fewer reporting requirements to put more emphasis on a better quality of report and improved compliance. It appeared that a number of the registered insurers were failing to deliver some of the most basic reports, like financial accounts, as we shall discuss below.

---

[23] As per the web site of ASF, which we consulted on 31/04/2018: http://www.asf.com.pt/NR/exeres/45EABD3E-0ACA-4FBA-B46E-53CD860B2A1E.htm

[24] Abbreviation for *Autoridade de Supervisão de Seguros e Fundos de Pensões*

## What were the required standards for financial accounting and reporting in Angola?

It was obligatory for all insurance companies to account for and report on their business in accordance with a local chart of accounts (*plano de contas*) as approved in decree no. 79.A/2002 of 5 December 2002 (art. 2). This obligatory chart of accounts was based on the standard of generally accepted accounting principles (GAAP). We were aware that one of the key global development trends in insurance markets was the shift to international financial reporting standards (IFRS). At the end of June 2018, only the banking sector in Angola had started applying IFRS (AXCO, 2018: 35). We believed that lawmakers could take advantage of the planned reform of the insurance regulatory framework to consider modernising local accounting models through adoption of IFRS standards, in alignment with global trends.

We observed that according to the General Law of Insurance, insurers were required to submit to the insurance regulator accounts at the end of the financial year, ending 31 December (Ch. III, s. IV, sub-s. IV, art. 37). These accounts were supposed to be submitted for each year by the 31st of March for the previous year. As specified in the General Law of Insurance, it was obligatory for the Insurance Regulator to clear the same accounts before their publication (Ch. III, s. IV, sub-s. IV, art. 37, cl. 2).

Notwithstanding this clear obligatory reporting condition, it appeared that some of the insurers were not publishing their annual accounts as required by the law. This appeared to be the situation of a handful of insurers. For instance, according to records of company registrations published by the Insurance Regulator, an insurer known as Mandume Seguros was supposed to have completed its registration process as far back as May 2012. However, financial information of this company was not included in the Angolan insurance market report for the period 2011 to 2013 (ARSEG, 2015: 94). We should highlight that failure to prepare accounting reports and to submit to the Insurance Regulator within the time limits defined in the Insurance Legal Framework was one of the legal infractions identified in the sanctions regime (ch. II, s. I, art. 3, cl. 1).

# 5.4 INTERNAL CONFLICT RESOLUTION MECHANISM

## What were the key procedures and requirements for handling complaints?

Roles and regulations for handling of complaints by insurance companies and pension fund administration companies were defined in regulatory notice no. 1/15 of 13 October 2015. According to this regulation (Ch. I, art. 4), each of the concerned entities was required to setup a complaints centre (*centro de reclamações*) and appoint a customer ombudsman (*provedor do cliente*). The service of this internal ombudsman to the clients was supposed to be free of charge, and it was not intended to prevent their right of recourse to court or other conflict resolution mechanisms (ch. I, art. 5). In addition, the complaints centres were required to submit reports to the regulator as and when requested (ch. II, art. 6).

The customer ombudsman could be an individual or collective entity, provided that there was no conflict of interest (ch. II, art. 13). As part of compliance requirements for the customer ombudsman, insurers and pension-fund administration companies were required to establish operational regulations as defined in the regulatory legislation (ch. II, art. 16). In order to ensure that complaints would be attended to in a timely fashion, the regulatory notice stipulated time limits for defined actions. However, the limits specified in different sections of the same regulatory notice were not the same. In one section of the notice, it was stated that companies were supposed to acknowledge receipt of all complaints within five days and respond within fifteen days for normal cases or twenty days for complex complaints (ch. II, art. 10). In another part of the same notice, it was specified that there should be written responses to complaints within twenty days from date of reception or thirty days for more complex claims (ch. II, art. 17). There was no definition of what constituted a complex case.

Finally, we noted that following the passing of this legislation in 2015, all concerned companies were supposed to notify the regulator of the setting up of the required mechanisms for handling of complaints within a period of ten days after their establishment (ch. III, art. 18). It was not clear how many companies had actually complied with this regulatory legislation since there were no public reports on these entities and their activities. We believed that this was one of the strictest forms of regulation of complaints in African insurance markets. We found that internal dispute resolution could be supplemented with an autonomous external mechanism. We also suggested that establishment of a formal insurance dispute resolution mechanism would support and ensure effectiveness of the internal mechanisms as per existing legislation.

## 5.5 OTHER KEY LEGAL PROVISIONS

### What changes of an insurance company required prior authorization?

The General Law of Insurance made provisions for certain forms of changes in an insurance company that required official authorization before implementation. The minister of finance was supposed to provide the required authorisation if everything was in order and subject to prior clearance by the insurance regulator. As specified in the General Law of Insurance, the following were the changes that required authorization (ch. III, s. V, art. 38, cl. 1):

- change of corporate name
- change of capital
- merger
- demerger or transfer of majority shareholding

Transfers of insurance and reinsurance portfolios were also subject to prior authorization for the regulator (ch. III, s. V, art. 38, cl. 3). If the portfolio to be transferred was life business, there should also be written agreement by at least 20 per cent of the insured persons (ch. III, s. V, art. 38, cl. 4).

### Under what circumstances should companies be liquidated?

According to the General Law of Insurance, companies in the following situations were supposed to be immediately placed under liquidation (ch. III, s. V, art. 39, cl. 1):

- insurers that had been dissolved
- insurers with licenses that had been withdrawn

In the case of extrajudicial liquidation, the insurance regulator had the authority to determine the period within which this process was supposed to be completed with approval of the final accounts and the liquidators' report. It was also stipulated in the same law of insurance that insurers under liquidation should not underwrite new business, renew or extend period of existing covers, or increase respective sums (ch. III, s. V, art. 39, cl. 3). We believed that, in principle, these were appropriate rules to protect consumers. However, it was important also to ensure appropriate mechanisms to monitor the financial soundness of the licensed entities and for the rules to be implemented in an impartial manner for all identified cases.

# 5.6 NON-ADMITTED INSURERS

## Could non-admitted insurers underwrite business in Angola?

The General Law of Insurance of Angola did not have provisions for the concept of non-admitted insurers. The insurance law clearly stated that insurance in Angola could only be underwritten by authorised and locally established insurers (ch. I, art. 3). In addition, it was clearly stated that insurance contracts with unauthorised insurers were not legally enforceable in Angola and could not be admitted in Angola courts (ch. I, art. 9, cl. 1). It was further stated in the same clause that sentences regarding such contracts were also not enforceable in Angola, even if a foreign court were to pass judgement on them.

The lack of validity of insurance contracts issued by unauthorised insurers for risks situated in Angola was reinforced in the Regulations on Conditions of Access and Conduct of Business of Insurers (ch. VII, art. 32 and 33). In this regulatory legislation, it was stated that such insurance contracts were null and void (*nulos e de nenhum efeito*). We have also noted that the sanctions regime of Angola, as defined in decree no. 7/02 of 9 April 2002, had reserved the highest level of fine regarding violation of this specific legal condition (ch. IV, art. 8).

## Was cross-border insurance permitted in Angola?

We noted that the African Insurance Regulatory Directory (2015: 41) stated that cross-border insurance was permitted in Angola, but it had 'to be shared with the local players'. From our review of the Angolan insurance regulatory framework, we have found no direct reference to the specific concept of cross-border insurance. We tend to agree with the observation from the CEO of the Insurance Regulatory Authority (IRA) of Kenya who was quoted in the same report as saying that the majority of African insurance market do not support the idea of cross-border insurance. Instead, they tended to 'advocate market protection and nationalism' (2015: 26).

As we discussed in the previous section of this chapter, it was very clear to us that a risk domiciled in Angola was not supposed to be insured directly by a foreign insurer, unless there was a specific exemption. However, we were also aware that there could be placement of a risk abroad at the reinsurance stage. In such an approach, one or more authorised insurers in Angola could underwrite a risk as inward insurance business and then place part of it as facultative reinsurance with a selected panel of reinsurance securities. Such reinsurance could only be done abroad (cross-border) for Angola, since there was not yet a local reinsurance market.

As per current practices in the region and in international markets, reinsurance capacity could be provided either by professional reinsurance companies or by global insurance companies with underwriting capacity to accept inward facultative reinsurance. Therefore, in our view, direct cross-border insurance or co-insurance with an unauthorised foreign insurer was not permitted, unless specific exemptions were granted by the appropriate authorities, as we shall discuss in the next topic. Foreign or cross-border reinsurance was permitted, provided that there was an underlying local insurance policy.

## What were the cases in which the insurance regulator could grant authorization for a local risk to be insured abroad?

Although insurers not registered in Angola could not directly issue policies for risks domiciled in this territory, the insurance regulator had the power to authorise insurance abroad in certain specific cases. According to the General Law of Insurance (Art. 9, Cl. 3), insurance abroad could be authorised in cases where the Angolan insurers would have declined to underwrite the risk and where there would have been authorization by the insurance regulator for placement abroad.

Furthermore, we noted that such exemptions were subject to additional rules as specified in the Regulations on Conditions of Access and Conduct of Business of Insurers (ch. VII, art. 32). It was stated that the entity seeking such an exemption to place abroad was supposed to apply for clearance with a minimum time period of fifteen days before the intended date of placement. The applicant was required to present justification for the application for exemption and provide proof of settlement of respective stamp tax and parafiscal levies applicable for insurance business

From this legal condition, it appeared that in this specific situation, a non-admitted insurer could be permitted to underwrite a risk in Angola without having to channel the risk via a registered local insurer. At the time of writing this case study, we were not aware of any foreign insurer that had been authorised to underwrite any risk in Angola. However, we were also aware that, due to a lack of an effective mechanism of ensuring compliance, there could be cases of insurers trying to underwrite risks outside their legal jurisdiction. We believed that some of the emerging global governance standards, such as the anti-money-laundering framework, were going to assist in preventing, amongst other things, violations of these types of rules and regulations on legal capacity of the insurer.

## What were the rules regarding setting up of branches?

We observed that the insurance legal framework of Angola contained rules regarding the need for insurers to have branches and to report on their activities. Insurers were supposed to have a minimum of three provincial branches in order to ensure appropriate service in the national territory, as specified in the Regulations to Streamline the Current Conditions for Accessing and Operating in the Insurance Market, as covered in executive decree no. 74/07 of 29 June 2007 (art. 3).

Besides the regulation specifying a minimum number of branches, as noted above, we have seen that there was a requirement for more extensive representation in the country for insurers intending to underwrite WCA insurance. In the legal framework of WCA insurance, as we shall discuss in Chapter 8, insurers were expected to have representation in all provincial cities, either in the form of a branch or of a local correspondent where they might not have a branch (ch. IV, art. 8, cl. 5 & 6). This meant that insurers doing this type of business were required to have representation in at least eighteen locations across the country, as per the map of the provinces in Angola illustrated in Figure 7.

**Figure 7: Provinces of Angola**

Source: Wikipedia https://upload.wikimedia.org/wikipedia/commons/b/be/Angola_Provinces_numbered_300px.png [Accessed 14 May 2018]

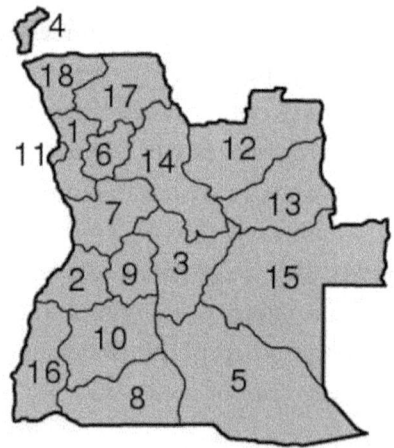

## Was there any reference to captives in the insurance legislative framework?

In our review of the current insurance legal framework of Angola, we did not see any reference to captive insurance or reinsurance entities. However, we noted that at least one of the insurance company had access to a captive structure registered in Bermuda. According to published accounts of AAA Reinsurance Ltd, all the business assumed by this company was underwritten through AAA Seguros in Angola (2017: 7). We shall discuss in Chapter 8 the financial impact on this captive following the changes of leadership of the oil and gas business from AAA to ENSA.

## Were there any rated companies in Angola?

A growing number of insurance companies in major regional markets in Africa found it necessary to have their financial strength assessed and rated by independent rating agencies. In the Angolan insurance market, we were aware of only two insurers that had credit ratings. Part of the reason for most of the insurers in Angola—and most countries in Africa—was connected to the issues of sovereign rating in the territories where they were located. Many African countries, including Angola, had poor ratings due to economic fundamentals. In accordance with existing global credit-rating frameworks, poor sovereign rating in any territory would adversely affect the rating of financial institutions based there. We saw indications of this sensitivity to sovereign rating in the reviews of rating of NOSSA, which was one of very few companies in Africa with an international credit rating (Fitch Ratings, 2018). The outlook of the rating of the company was positively reviewed in alignment with that of the country at the end of the half of 2018, following application of measures by the new government to improve performance of the economy.

Notwithstanding the challenges noted above, we found that the process of rating was a vital element in ascertaining the strength of the financial markets and giving consumers confidence. The types of scrutiny done by these agencies was at a far superior level to any of the monitoring that could be done by the regulatory authorities—especially in Africa, where many already had challenges of limited skills and resources. Furthermore, financial credit rating had been adopted as one of the key risk-management requirements to determine financial service providers for operators in megaprojects and major operations in areas such as mining, aviation, construction, oil, and gas.

## 5.7 OTHER PREOCCUPATIONS

From our experience of attempting to register an insurance company in Angola, we found that it was not possible to know clearly all the requirements upfront. There was also no clarity as to the time it would take to set up. Investors interested in setting up business in Angola needed to consult extensively on all the rules and regulations for establishing and doing business there before beginning the investment process. This sort of problem was not unique to Angola. It tended to be a major challenge for doing business in most of the countries in Africa. We believed that it would be beneficial for subregional groupings such as SADC to consider plans to harmonise regulatory frameworks and improve ease of doing business.

Following our review of the overall legal framework that had to be followed by all companies doing insurance business in Angola and the laws for the financial sector in general, we shall now focus on insurance and reinsurance intermediation.

# References

AIO (2017), *Africa Insurance Barometer 2017*, Zurich: Schanz, Alms, and Company AG: Zurich.

Angop (2017), 'Angola Stock Exchange May Play Strategic Role in SADC', http://www.angop.ao/angola/en_us/noticias/economia/2017/2/11/Angola-Stock-Exchange-may-play-strategic-role-SADC, f9423b85-4a9c-4008-951a-0674cb75d222.html (accessed 11 May 2018).

ARSEG, *Fundo de Actualização e Regularização de Seguros (FUNSEG)* http://www.arseg.ao/index.php?option=com_content&view=article&id=127&Itemid=180&lang=pt [Accessed on 16/05/2018]

AXCO (2018), *Angola: Non-Life Insurance Market Report*. London: AXCO Insurance Information Services.

BODIVA (2015), 'Relatório e Contas 2015', http://www.bodiva.ao/files/relatorio-contas/relatorio-e-contas-2015.pdf [accessed 11/05/2018]

Fitch Ratings (2018). Fitch Revises Nova Sociedade de Seguros de Angola's Outlook to Stable; Affirms IFS at 'B' https://www.fitchratings.com/site/pr/10029450 [Accessed 28 May 2018]

NOSSA (2017) 'Relatório e Contas Anual 2017', http://www.nossaseguros.ao/uploads/widgets/20/201812281542515c26447be432b.pdf [Accessed 26 March 2019]

# Chapter 6

# INTERMEDIATION OF INSURANCE AND REINSURANCE

Following our review of the key basic conditions for registering and doing insurance business in Angola, we will now look at the rules and regulations for intermediation of the insurance and reinsurance business. Insurance intermediation was one of the key drivers of growth of insurance, and it was a vital channel for increasing awareness of insurance and supporting consumer confidence (de Abreu, 2014: 317). It was also a key mechanism for promoting competition in the insurance sector. As noted by McCord (2008: 357), insurance agents (one of the forms of intermediaries) have been in existence '[f]or as long as there had been insurance'—from the early days of commercialisation of insurance in the Industrial Age.

An intermediary could be defined as a firm or individual that served as a go-between with the intention of offering to provide some service between two parties that were trying to exchange something. Intermediaries offered this service for a fee that could be provided by the supplier or buyer of the service or good under consideration. Intermediaries could be found in businesses such as the stock exchange, sales of property, insurance, and other areas. However, the concept of an intermediary was more widely practiced in the insurance business than other activity given the complexities of insurance contracts (Mathonsi, 2013: 5). According to Nazaré (2008: 137), intermediaries served as the connecting link (*elo de ligação*) between the insured and the insurer and made a significant impact in the growth and development of insurance.

# 6.1 INSURANCE INTERMEDIATION

The conditions of accessing and conducting the business of insurance intermediation was covered in the General Law of Insurance and respective regulations. The regulations for intermediaries are covered in executive decree no. 7/03 of 24 January 2003[25] (de Abreu, 2014: 308–316). We shall refer to this specific piece of regulatory legislation as the regulations of insurance intermediaries. In addition, we shall take into account the following regulatory legislation with key legal conditions for intermediaries:

- circular no. 06/ISS.MF/10 of 2 August 2010 on insurance intermediation
- executive decree no. 465/16 of 1 December 2016—Update of Fines in Respect of Infringement of the Regulations Relating to Insurance Agencies and Brokerage as Approved in Executive Decree no. 7/03 of 24 January 2003.

The directives from the insurance regulator as per the circular no. 06/ISS/MF/10 of 2 August 2010 contained further regulations in respect of insurance intermediation.

## Who had legal capacity to do insurance intermediation in Angola?

According to the General Law of Insurance, like insurance underwriting, intermediation of insurance in Angola was to only be done by entities authorized by Angolan authorities to set up in accordance with the conditions defined in this law (ch. 1, art. 3, cl. 1). Furthermore, as defined in the Regulations of Insurance Intermediaries, there were the following types of authorised intermediaries (ch. I, art. 4):

- individual tied agent (*angariador de seguros*[26])
- insurance agent (*agente de seguros*)
- insurance brokerage (*corretor de seguros*)

Please note that we did not follow the order of the list as per the regulations. We chose to follow the order of their hierarchy in the practice

---

[25] Referred to in Portuguese as *Decreto Executivo nº 7/03 de 24 de Janeiro*
[26] Also referred to as '*mediador de seguro ligado*' by Leiria (2013: 198)

of intermediation, starting from the simplest form of intermediary to the highest level of intermediation as a broker. The key distinguishing features of these types of intermediaries, as defined in the regulatory framework, were as outlined in Table 7.

**Table 7: Types of Local Insurance Intermediaries in Angola**

| | Type of Intermediary | Nature of Agency | Minimum Personnel | Professional Indemnity Insurance |
|---|---|---|---|---|
| 1 | Tied Agent | Exclusive | Not Specified | Not Obligatory |
| 2 | Insurance Agent | Independent | Not Specified | Not Obligatory |
| 3 | Insurance Broker | Independent | 5 members of staff | Minimum $100,000 |

## What were the conditions for an individual to register as an insurance intermediary?

According to the Regulations of Insurance Intermediaries, an individual intending to be an insurance intermediary should be registered with the insurance regulator through an insurance company (ch. II, art. 5). The person applying to be registered had to satisfy the following conditions:

a) legal age - in accordance with the Civil Law of Angola, the legal age was 18 years or older.

b) legal capacity to conduct business

c) possession of minimum academic qualifications of middle level of schooling as per the official education system and/or an adequate level of professional qualifications to practice insurance business

d) resident of Angola

e) not employed or temporarily retired from insurance business

f) not convicted for any of the following crimes: theft, burglary, breach of trust, fraud, embezzlement, fraudulent falsehood or breach, or any other fraudulent offences qualifying for a prison sentence

g) passed technical and professional tests for intermediaries to qualify for a certificate of insurance intermediation (*certificado de mediador*) as per the model presented in the same regulatory regulations

It was stated in the regulations that criteria e) noted above did not apply to tied agents, since these could be employed by the insurer (ch. II, art. 5, cl. 2). We believed that this exemption could create space for conflict of interest of employees in insurers earning commission on books of business underwritten by their employer. From our experience in Mozambique, one of the fears of independent brokers and agents was that a tied agent serving as an underwriter in an insurer could frustrate their efforts to be nominated as intermediaries on business where the underwriter was also earning commissions.

## Were qualifications from professional insurance institutes accepted?

There was no reference in the General Law of Insurance and the respective regulations to the question of qualifications from professional Insurance Institutes in the region or in international markets. At the time of writing this book, there was no professional insurance institute in Angola. Furthermore, we noted that there could be exemptions from the examination process for registration of an individual as an intermediary. According to the circular on intermediation, no. 06/ISS/MF/10, an individual could obtain an exemption if there was an insurer or an appropriate individual who could testify that the applicant in question had proven experience and professional standing in the insurance sector (ch. I, art. 3). It was not clear how this procedure was supposed to be handled and all the respective requirements for such an individual. The circular only specified that the individual in question was supposed to be an Angolan citizen or a foreigner who had been a resident in Angola for a minimum of five years.

## What were the conditions for a corporate entity to register as an insurance intermediary?

All corporate entities intending to serve as insurance intermediaries were required to register with the insurance regulator and were supposed to satisfy all of the following conditions as outlined in the Regulations of Insurance Intermediaries (ch. II, art. 5):

a) The corporate entity was appropriately registered as a private limited company (*sociedade por quota*) or a public limited company (*sociedade anónima*).

b) The corporate purpose (*objecto social*) of the company in question was exclusively insurance intermediation.

c) The directors (*administradores*) and managers of the intermediary were not directors or active employees or in a situation of provisional retirement in an insurance company.

d) The shareholders (*sócios*), directors, and managers had never been convicted of theft, burglary, breach of trust, fraud, embezzlement, fraudulent falsehood or breach, or any other fraudulent offences which would qualify for a prison sentence.

e) The directors and managers of the intermediary were not persons who had been declared bankrupt.

f) The insurance intermediary company had among its employees, managers, or directors at least one person registered as an insurance intermediary. As noted in our review of registration of individuals for the certificate of insurance intermediaries, this includes passing a specific technical and professional insurance intermediaries test of the insurance regulator.

g) There was proof of economic viability of the intended insurance intermediary company.

As of 30 June 2018, there were fifty-six insurance intermediary companies registered in Angola, as outlined in Appendix V. We also observed that most of the insurance intermediaries were registered as private limited companies. From this list, only ten of the registered entities were public limited companies.

## What were rules for registration of a foreigner as an insurance intermediary?

According to the **Regulations of Insurance Intermediaries**, foreign citizens that had been resident in Angola for at least five years could qualify to apply for registration as insurance intermediaries in Angola, provided that their country of origin offered reciprocal conditions for

Angolan citizens (ch. II, art. 8, cl. 1). This regulation was connected to the legal principle of reciprocity as provided for in the General Law of Insurance (Ch. V, art. 41, cl. 3). Furthermore, the foreign citizen could only qualify for registration subject to satisfying all the conditions in respect of registration of individuals and corporate entities as insurance intermediaries, as discussed above.

## On what basis could the license of an intermediary expire or be cancelled?

As specified in Regulations of Insurance Intermediaries, the license of an insurance intermediary could expire under the following circumstances (ch. II, art. 9, cl. 1):
- death of an individual insurance intermediary
- liquidation of the intermediary corporate entity

The same regulations stipulated that the license of an intermediary could be cancelled following an express request from the respective intermediary (ch. II, art. 9, cl. 2). Insurance agents or insurance brokers intending to cancel their licenses were required to submit the request directly to the insurance regulator. For tied agents (*angariadores*), as discussed above, authorizations were secured through an insurance company. Therefore, their request for cancellation was supposed to be channelled through the insurer through whom the license was secured.

## How was a tied insurance agent defined in the insurance legislation?

According to the Regulations of Insurance Intermediaries, a tied insurance agent was an individual working as an insurance intermediary for an insurance company and appropriately licensed in accordance with the rules and regulations of this same piece of legislation (ch. III, s. II, art. 13, cl. 1). Tied agents were required to operate exclusively for the insurer through whom they were licensed for all business unless handling classes of insurance for which the insurer to which they were tied was not underwriting (ch. III, s. II, art. 13, cl. 1). In addition, it was stipulated in the regulations that insurers proposing agents for registration had the responsibility to provide training for their tied agents before putting forward their names for the qualification tests with the insurance regulator (ch. III, s. II, art. 13, cl. 3). We should also note that as provided for in the Regulations of Insurance Intermediaries, Article 15 of the same section, a tied agent could upgrade to the next level of an insurance agent (ch. III, s. II, art. 15).

Finally, we should point out that some insurance market observers had concerns about this system where insurers had tied agents working for them and potentially targeting the same clients that independent insurance agents and insurance brokers wanted to serve. According to de Abreu (2014: 317), conflict of interest could arise in the interaction of an insurer that had tied agents that could have access to information on the portfolio of the insurer, including business from the independent intermediaries. This concept could have become outdated following the opening up of the insurance market and the emerging approach of promotion of free competition.

## What was the official definition of an insurance agent?

As defined in the Regulations of Insurance Intermediaries, an insurance agent was an intermediary authorized as such by the insurance regulator, and that could be an individual or a corporate entity (ch. III, s. I, art. 10). Insurance agents could search for insurance business in the market and provide assistance on insurance agreements underwritten through their intervention. Insurance agents could also be responsible for collection of premiums from their insurance clients.

## What was the process for certification of an insurance agent?

According to the Regulations of Insurance Intermediaries, applicants for licensing as insurance agents would go through an assessment test conducted by a panel (*júri*) consisting of three insurance professionals nominated by the insurance regulator (ch. III, s. I, art. 11). The insurance regulator should serve as the chairman of this panel. As specified in the same section of the law, only insurance companies could propose names of individuals for this qualifying examination. For those who failed, it was possible to apply for re-examination. The candidates who passed this test would qualify for registration as independent insurance agents. Such types of qualified independent agents could serve as intermediaries for any of the insurance companies in the market.

We should note that the status of autonomy was one of the key distinguishing features between insurance agents and tied agents. We should also note that this agent certification was a crucial item for the licensing of a corporate entity as an insurance agency company or as an insurance brokerage firm. As we saw in the registration process of companies as agents or brokers, at least one member of staff of the corporate entity was supposed to be a certified insurance intermediary.

## What was the definition of an insurance broker in the insurance legislation of Angola?

As per the definition in the Regulations of Insurance Intermediaries, an insurance broker (*corretor de seguros*) was a corporate entity authorized to do the business activity of insurance intermediation (ch. III, s. III, art. 16). A broker was supposed to prepare for signing of insurance agreements and assist insured parties. A broker could also provide insurance advice, conduct analysis of insurance, and provide technical opinions.

## How was an insurance broker to be remunerated?

As stated in the Regulations of Insurance Intermediaries on insurance intermediation (ch. III, s. III, art. 17), an insurance broker was entitled to remuneration in the form insurance brokerage commission (*comissão de corretagem*). In addition to commission, brokers could charge a fee for insurance consultation, studies, and technical opinions. From our inquiry with our contacts in Angola, we were informed that there were no uniform intermediary commission rates in the market. We would like to also note that for health insurance in particular, some insurers followed a model involving appointment of a third-party administrator (TPA). In such cases, the insurers would pay a fee to these entities. We were of the opinion that it would be important for appropriate rules and regulations for this type of entity to be defined in the insurance regulatory framework.

## What were the conditions for registration of an insurance broker?

As per the rules specified in the Regulations of Insurance Intermediaries, only corporate entities could be registered as insurance brokers (ch. III, s. III, art. 18). Entities intending to register as insurance brokerage companies were required to do the following:

- set up as a company with appropriate commercial and administrative organization
- have five active staff members for at least two years
- have at least one risk analyst
- meet all other conditions of registration of a corporate entity as an intermediary, as discussed above

## What were the capital requirements for intermediaries?

According to Regulations of Insurance Intermediaries, the following was the minimum capital required for each different type of insurance intermediaries (ch. IV, art. 19):

- tied agent: not specified, since this type of intermediary is registered on the basis of the license of an insurer
- insurance agent: $20,000
- insurance broker: $50,000
- reinsurance broker: $150,000
- insurance and reinsurance broker: $200,000[27]

We observed that these minimum capital requirements were not revised following their setting in 2003 at the time of the passing of the Regulations of Insurance Intermediaries. We had observed that the insurance regulator focused on revising upwards the amount of capitalisation for only insurance companies. We believed that with the planned reforms of the insurance regulatory framework, there could also be a review of capital requirements for intermediaries.

---

[27] This was the sum of the minimum Capital of US$ 50,000 for an insurance broker as specified in the Regulations of Insurance Intermediaries and the minimum capital of $150,000 for a reinsurance broker as specified in the Regulations on Reinsurance and Coinsurance.

## What were the duties of an insurance intermediary?

According to the Regulations of Insurance, the duties of an intermediary consisted of the following (ch. VI, art. 25):

- presenting to the insured details of the product and type of contract that were most appropriate for their specific situation
- advising the insurer of the risks to be covered and their respective risk details
- advising the insurer of any changes arising on insured risks that they may become aware of and that may have an influence on the term and conditions of the respective policies.
- ensuring compliance with all legal conditions and in particular those in respect of insurance business
- not assuming cover of risks in their own name
- providing to the insured only services in respect of their business activity of insurance intermediation
- maintaining confidentiality from third parties facts that they could become aware of as a result of doing their business of insurance intermediation
- disclosing all facts that they were aware of that could have an impact on settlement of a claim
- submitting accounts to the insurer in accordance with the terms and conditions of the intermediation service agreement which was required as specified in the Insurance Intermediation Regulations (ch. I, art. 3, cl. 2)
- not granting commissions to the client, third parties, or other brokers, and not granting any premium discount in any form
- collecting premiums on all invoices received and send back to the insurer in all cases where there was no collection
- collaborating with the insurer on claims settlement, subject to this being provided for in their respective intermediation agreement

We would like to note that in addition to all the duties of intermediaries in general as outlined above, an insurance broker was subject to particular obligations as stipulated in ch. VII, art. 25, cl. 2. We shall not discuss all the additional duties specified for brokers. We would like to focus on one of the key requirements for professional indemnity insurance, as noted below.

## Was professional indemnity insurance obligatory for intermediaries?

Professional indemnity insurance (*seguro de responsabilidade civil profissional*) was specified as one of the additional obligations for insurance and reinsurance brokers in the Regulations of Insurance Intermediaries. This was a critical legal requirement given that professional indemnity was intended to provide insurance protection for individuals and firms that provided advice and professional service (Vaughan, 2009: 481). The standard policy was supposed to cover the following situations:

- negligence, errors, omissions, misrepresentation, and misstatement
- unintentional breach of confidentiality, trust, authority, or privacy
- defamation
- accidental loss or damage of third-party documents and property entrusted to the professional
- violation of good faith and fair dealing

All the risks noted above were highly sensitive in the activity of insurance intermediation. We believed that it was crucial for the regulatory framework to specify the scope of cover for such types of policies. In the current Regulations of Insurance Intermediaries of Angola, the minimum amount of required covers were as follows:

- insurance brokers: $100,000 (ch. VII, art. 25, cl. 2g)
- reinsurance brokers: $200,000 (ch. VII, art. 25, cl. 2h)

We were of the opinion that these were very low limits in comparison to the potential exposure for intermediaries if they were to have major claims. We had observed that tender projects from most multinational companies operating in Africa demanded cover of $10 million or more. We believed that the limits of cover for professional indemnity needed to be increased significantly in the proposed reform exercise of the insurance regulatory framework.

## Could there be more than one broker on one insurance policy?

We were aware that in most African markets, there could be more than one broker on any one insurance policy. In such cases, there could

94

be a flag broker as the principal intermediary and supporting brokers also earning commissions on the same account. According to the Regulations of Insurance Intermediaries of Angola, each insurance policy was supposed to have only one intermediary (ch. VII, art. 30). However, there was an exception in contracts involving coinsurance, where there could be a broker for each of the shares of the coinsurers.

It was not clear to us if this rule was also intended to prevent the prevalent practice of global brokers collaborating with local correspondent brokers on their accounts in territories where they did not have local licenses. Such global brokers controlled most of the major multinational accounts. They would sign global service agreements with their clients and try to guarantee service in all the areas where the clients might choose to invest. We believed that these global operators would always find ways to appoint local correspondents and set up arrangements to share commissions and fees.

## For which type of insurance was payment of commission to intermediaries not permitted?

Besides the issue noted above, there was one major restriction that affected the business of insurance intermediation in the key economic sectors of Angola. According to the Regulations of Insurance Intermediaries insurance intermediation regulations (ch. VII, art. 31) and circular on intermediation (ch. IV, art. 11), payment of commission to intermediaries was not permitted for the following types of insurance business:

- obligatory types of insurance
- special types of business subject to obligatory coinsurance, as defined in decree no. 6/01 of 2 March 2001, as we shall discuss in Chapter 10.
- insurance contracts of the national and local governments as well as public entities

We shall discuss further legal references later in this book regarding the restriction of commissions on obligatory types of insurance. We should note that the second item relates to the oil and gas business as well as other major types of insurance that were subject to compulsory coinsurance.

From our experience of underwriting this type of business, global brokerage firms played a critical role in the conceptualization, designing, placing, servicing, and administration of such accounts. If anything, this was the area where advice and service of insurance brokers was needed the most. We were also aware that it was very rare for intermediaries to earn standard commission rates for this type of business due to the very high volumes of business involved. In most cases, intermediaries on these risks earned only a fixed fee. Normally, their clients would require them to sign agreements giving back any commissions paid by insurers back to the client. In the majority of cases that we saw in Angola, the brokers would also control the pricing at the reinsurance level. As such, the broker could instruct the insurer to issue on a free of commissions basis and then collect a fee directly from the client.

## Was there an Intermediaries Guarantee Fund in Angola?

From our review of the insurance legal framework of Angola, we have not been able to identify a mechanism to protect premium received by intermediaries on behalf of insurers. In our book on the insurance market of Mozambique, we noted that this was one of the key conditions for safeguarding payments through insurance intermediaries (Muchena, 2018: 177). Most insurance markets in Africa do not have such facilities. One of the best examples of appropriate mechanisms was the Intermediaries Guarantee Fund (IGF) of South Africa, as we were able to review from their website.[28]

Given that most countries in Africa were following macroeconomic policies where they tended to avoid setting up too many public funds, one could also look at alternative models. For instance, according to the insurance regulator in Portugal (ASF, 2007: 131), insurance brokers were required to provide protection of premium through an insurance guarantee (*caução de seguro*) or a bank guarantee (*garantia bancária*). This kind of private financial market-based option could be considered for Angola, Mozambique, and other insurance markets as part of the mechanism of improving consumer protection.

---

[28] http://www.igfsec45.co.za/#!/ (accessed on 29 June 2018)

# 6.2 BANCASSURANCE AND OTHER CHANNELS

One of the major preoccupations with regards to insurance intermediation was the lack of effective channels of insurance distribution. While professional insurance brokers and agents have the knowledge to provide required intermediation services, they lack the means to enable access to insurance products and services to mass markets. As a result of this realization of the limitations of traditional intermediaries, there had been a growing trend of exploration of new channels, including bancassurance, mobile telephones, and retail distribution (Leiria, 2013: 202–207). Bancassurance could be defined as 'the joint effort of banks and insurers to provide insurance services to the bank's customer base' (Swiss Re, 2007: 5). Besides bancassurance, we could not identify any major initiatives in Angola involving exploration of new distribution channels.

## Was bancassurance permitted in Angola?

We would like begin by noting that we could not find in the current insurance legislation specific provisions in respect of bancassurance or distribution of insurance through channels of banking institutions. However, we observed that there was a reference to this form of intermediation in the Financial Institutions Law no. 12/2015 of 17 June 2015. According to this law, banks were permitted to do insurance intermediation (ch. I, art. 6, cl. 1j). There was no clarification in this law and in the insurance regulations as to whether all the contemporary models of bancassurance were permitted. We should note that a number of registered insurance companies were either part of banking groups or had signed bancassurance agreements.

Furthermore, we would like to note that it was crucial for insurance regulation to provide more guidelines on this question, given the growing dominance of investment of banks in insurance and partnerships with existing insurers in Angola and other African markets interested in increasing retail distribution of insurance. From our review of global bancassurance, we noted that the key approaches were as follows:

- **Pure Distributor**—In this model, a bank acted like a conventional insurance intermediary or broker that could distribute insurance products from different insurance companies in the market. When a bank would choose this model, the personnel involved in the handling of insurance needed to have enough training in insurance to be able to provide appropriate advice to their clients in choosing between different products from different service providers.

- **Exclusive Cooperation Agreement**—In this case, the bank was expected to focus exclusively on distributing a specified range of insurance from only one insurance company. This model tended not to demand the same levels of skill and knowledge in insurance as the option noted above. This tended to be the preferred model for bancassurance models in Mozambique (Muchena: 2018, 147).
- **Joint Venture**—A bank and an insurer would create together a separate entity to distribute insurance products.
- **Vertical Integration**—This was an approach based on a classical economic concept of integration. The bank would acquire an insurance license in order to directly align interests and grow a range of services to its client-base.
- **Fully Integrated Model**—Here, banking and insurance services were fully integrated. The personnel and systems would need to be fully geared to handle all the needs of the client for both banking and insurance through the same channels.

## Were conditional sales prohibited in Angola?

This was a vital question to discuss, given the growing influence of banking institutions in the insurance sector of Angola as investors and as channels of insurance distribution. We did not find any specific reference to the concept of conditional sales in the current insurance legal framework. However, the Financial Institutions Law made it clear that conditional selling was prohibited (art. 85, cl. 1c).

## 6.3 REINSURANCE BROKERAGE

### Which reinsurance brokers were permitted to do business in Angola?

According to the Reinsurance and Coinsurance Regulations no. 6/01 of 2 March 2001 (Dias, 2012: 326 – 343), only reinsurance brokers registered with the Angolan insurance regulator were permitted to serve as reinsurance brokers for local reinsurance business (ch. II, art. 11). This registration was required for both local and foreign brokers.

We were aware that a number of registered local insurance brokers also had authorization to do reinsurance brokerage. However, we had not seen any of the local brokers handling the reinsurance treaty programmes of any of the insurance companies in Angola. We believed that there would probably be a risk of conflict of interest if the same brokerage firm were to try to control both the insurance intermediation placing business with insurers as well as the respective reinsurance of the same portfolio. We were also aware that for large risks in aviation, mining, oil, and gas, there had been a gradual blurring of the distinction between insurance and reinsurance intermediation.

### What was the minimum capital required for a reinsurance broker?

As per our discussions on insurance brokerage above, the minimum amount of paid-up capital for a local reinsurance broker was US$150,000, as defined in the Regulations of Insurance Intermediaries (ch. IV, art. 19). Furthermore, the minimum capital would be US$200,000 in the case of brokers that were licensed to do both insurance and reinsurance brokerage.

### How many reinsurance brokers were registered in Angola?

We have noted that fourteen of the 56 registered intermediaries were licensed to do both insurance and reinsurance business as per Appendix V. We were not aware of any brokers in Angola dedicated exclusively to reinsurance. Furthermore, the website of the insurance regulator did not provide a list of registered foreign reinsurance brokers doing business in Angola. We were aware that placement of virtually all the reinsurance treaty programmes of the local insurance companies was handled by foreign brokers, with the exception of a few direct placements.

# 6.4 REPORTING REQUIREMENTS FOR INTERMEDIARIES

## What were the key reporting conditions for insurance intermediaries?

There were a number of legal reporting requirements for insurance intermediaries in the insurance legal framework. Please see Appendix VI for a list of the key reporting requirements that we identified in the current insurance regulatory framework at the beginning of 2018. We would like to stress that this was not an exhaustive list of all the reporting requirements for a business entity. We recommend further consultation on this subject for people who may want to obtain a more up-to-date and comprehensive outline of all the reporting compliance requirements for businesses.

We have observed a number of reporting requirements in respect of insurance intermediaries in the current insurance legal framework. We also noticed that there appeared not to be appropriate reference material that would allow us to access all the key reporting conditions without having to check in every piece of legislation relating to insurance. We would like to recommend that for Angola, the regulatory authority could draw up an updated list of all the key reporting requirements for insurance intermediaries, as we observed on the website of ASF, the Insurance Regulator in Portugal (ASF, 2007).

Furthermore, we have noted that the sanctions regime in decree no. 7/02 of 9 April 2002 also provided for fines and penalties for failure to comply with the reporting requirements referred to above. The sanctions could be applied on both the registered intermediary business entity (ch. II, sub-s. I & II) and on the managers of the companies in their individual capacity (ch. II, sub-s. I & II). For serious offences by companies, there could be partial or total suspension of business activities or, worse still, cancellation of the license. For individuals, the sanctions could include prohibition from working in the insurance business for a defined period, depending on gravity of the offence.

# References

ASF (2007), *Relatório do Setor Segurador e dos Fundos de Pensões*, http://www.asf.com.pt/NR/exeres/9761BAC3-D3A7-4DEB-928C-C1FAAB73D544.htm (accessed 26/04/2018).

de Abreu, Ana Edith Viegas (2014), *100 Anos de Legislação de Seguros em Angola*. Luanda: Edições Chá de Caxinde.

Dias, Nélia Daniel (2012), *Legislação Financeira e dos Seguros*. Luanda: Texto Editores, Lda.

Leiria, Manuel (2013), *Marketing de Seguros*. Lisboa: Escola Editora

Mathonsi, George (2013), 'Cobrança e Canalização de Prémios às Seguradoras', paper presented at the Insurance Seminar of the ISSM.

McCord, Michael, J. (2008), 'The partner-agent model: Challenges and opportunities', in Churchill, Craig (ed.), *Protecting the Poor: A Microinsurance Compendium*. Geneva: International Labour Office, and Munic: the Munich Re Foundation, 357–377.

Muchena, Israel (2018), *Development of Insurance in Mozambique*. Bloomington: AuthorHouse

Nazaré, Domingas, Miguel (2008). A ENSA e a Reforma do Sector Seguradora em Angola. Luanda – Caxinde – Editora e Livraria

Swiss Re (2007), *Bancassurance: Emerging Trends, Opportunities and Challenges*, Sigma No. 5/2007. Zurich: Swiss Reinsurance Company Ltd.

Vaughan, Emmet J. (1992), *Fundamentals of Risk and Insurance*, 6th ed. New York: John Wiley and Sons Inc.

Chapter 7

# OBLIGATORY PRIVATE INSURANCE

Following our review in Chapter 4 of social insurance and other forms
of public insurance covered by the government or public funds, we shall
now look at the other forms of obligatory insurance covered by the private
insurance market in Angola. In our research on the current Angolan
insurance market, we identified at least eleven regulated types of obligatory
insurance that were supposed to be handled by the private insurance
market. We shall see how three of them are supported by appropriate
regulatory legislation whilst the rest appear not to have been appropriately
regulated at the time of our research.

We were able to obtain the bulk of our references on obligatory types
of insurance from the collection of legislation in the book *100 Anos de
Legislação de Seguros em Angola* (de Abreu, 2014: 437–489). We were also
able to obtain updates of the overall legislation on the highly informative
official website of Governo de Angola[29] as well as the website LexLink.[30] We
shall also discuss at the end of this chapter new types of obligatory insurance
that were currently being considered for adoption at the time of this writing.

## 7.1 WORKMEN'S COMPENSATION ACT INSURANCE

Workmen's Compensation Act insurance (*seguro de acidentes de
trabalho*) was an obligatory insurance intended to cover employees of an

---

[29] http://www.governo.gov.ao/TodasLegislacoes.aspx
[30] https://www.lexlink.eu/legislacao/angola/legal/tudo/por-tipo-de-documentolegal

insured entity against work-related accidents (*acidentes de trabalho*) and occupational illnesses (*doenças profissionais*). The legal framework for this insurance in Angola was provided for in decree no. 53/05 of 15 August 2005 (Achega, 2014: 667 – 690). We shall now discuss some of the key features of this obligatory type of insurance, which we shall refer to by its abbreviation: WCA insurance. We shall refer to the regulations for this class of business as the WCA insurance regulatory framework.

## Who should be covered by WCA Insurance?

As defined in the WCA insurance regulatory framework, it was obligatory to insure any person working for another party (*por conta outrem*) against the risks of work-related accidents and occupational illnesses (ch. I, art. 1). Angolan employees working for an Angolan company or organisation were also entitled to this cover when temporarily on mission or working abroad. unless if in the country where they would be located, they would have similar or better cover. Foreign workers residing in Angola were also to be covered on this obligatory policy.

Although it was not obligatory for self-employed workers (*trabalhadores por conta própria*) to insure in terms of this specific legislation, they could place this insurance for themselves. Nonresident foreign workers were also not required to have this insurance, provided they could demonstrate that they had a similar type of cover. Furthermore, WCA insurance was not intended to cover civil servants and public service workers. However, we have noted that according to the same legislation (ch. XIII, art. 57), before promulgation of appropriate regulations to cover civil servants and public service workers, they could be covered within the ambit of the current WCA insurance regulatory framework.

## What was the scope of cover of a WCA insurance policy?

As defined in the WCA insurance regulatory framework, this type of insurance was supposed to cover sudden and unforeseen work-related accidents (ch. II, art. 3) and occupational illnesses (ch. III, art. 6). The accident or illness was supposed to cause injury (*lesão*) or bodily damage (*danos corporais*) which resulted in the following events:

- partial or total temporary disability,
- permanent disability
- death

The definition of a covered accident in WCA insurance was also extended to cover that could occur under the following circumstances:
- in transit to and from work following the normal and usual routing
- during resting intervals at work,
- as a result of defending human lives and property at the premises of the insured entity
- during social, cultural, and sporting activities organised by the insured entity

## What were the key legal requirements for the underwriting of WCA insurance?

The WCA insurance law stipulated legal conditions to be observed in the underwriting of this form of insurance. The key conditions for underwriting of this type of policy, as defined in this piece of legislation (ch. IV, art. 8), were as follows:

a) WCA Insurance was subject to an obligatory tariff system for calculation of premiums. However, some market observers noted that not all insurers applied in all cases the minimum stipulated premium rates (AXCO, 2011: 6). We shall discuss the regulatory framework in respect of tariffs in Chapter 9.

b) On a half-yearly basis, insured employers were required to send to the insurer a copy of their monthly payroll (*folha de remunerações*), duly authenticated by the general inspectorate of labour (*inspecção-geral do trabalho*). We understand the need for this procedure in order to avoid the risk of under-declaration of salaries that we observed in our research in Mozambique. However, we also believed it would be useful for markets with this type of product to find effective and less bureaucratic ways to handle the declaration of salaries, as the basis for determining cost of insurance as well as the basis for compensation of victims of accidents.

c) The employer was prohibited from charging or sharing costs of WCA insurance with covered employees.

d) Insurance companies were prohibited from paying insurance brokerage for this class of business. This was in alignment with the conditions noted in the Insurance Intermediation Regulations in Chapter 6.

e) Insurers underwriting WCA insurance business were required to have nationwide representation. For any provincial capital cities where an insurer did not have an office, the insurer was expected to appoint a local correspondent and notify accordingly the respective provincial directorate of the social security scheme.

f) For any risk that was rejected by all insurers in the Angolan market, the social security authorities were supposed to designate an insurer that would be required to underwrite the policy in question.

g) Insurers underwriting WCA insurance were also required to submit half-yearly reports on this type of business to the National Directorate of Social Security. The reporting requirements were supposed to be defined in further regulatory legislation from both the Ministry of Finance and the authorities of social security.

Among the rules and regulations noted above, we noted that social security authorities had the power to instruct a designated insurer to underwrite a risk that would have been rejected by all the operators in the private insurance market. We were not aware if there existed a precedent for such a situation. However, we would like to observe that it would not be in alignment with the principles of private business for the authorities to try to interfere in the underwriting decisions of an insurer. We believed that in business, it was essential to always satisfy the condition of 'willing buyer, willing seller'.

## What was the special rule regarding cancellation of a WCA insurance contract?

We noted a critical legal condition in respect to the WCA insurance specified in the Regulations on Conditions of Access and Conduct of

Business of Insurers, executive decree no. 5/03 of 24 January 2003. The regulations stipulated that cancellation of a policy covering the obligatory WCA insurance required notification of both the insured employer and the supervisory body (*orgão de fiscalização*) for social security (ch. 30, art. 30, cl. 1). We understood the need for this reporting requirement, since this type of insurance was partly subject to supervision by the social security authority.

## Was there unlimited exposure in WCA insurance in Angola?

The WCA insurance regulations in Angola did not expressly state that insurers were required to issue policies with unlimited liability for this type of business. However, in practice, we noted that there was unlimited liability, since the policies issued by the market did not cap exposure like all the other risks underwritten by the insurance market. We believed that since the insurance companies in the private insurance market were limited liability companies, they were supposed to avoid assuming unlimited exposure. In addition, reinsurance markets supporting the insurance market did not provide unlimited capacity.

## What were the key conditions regarding occupational safety, hygiene, and health?

The regulations in respect of occupational safety, hygiene, and health (*segurança, hygiene e saúde no trabalho*) were established in decree no. 31/94 of 5 August 1994. We have noted that the key obligations for employers specified in these regulations included measures aimed at setting up an appropriate risk management framework in order to prevent or reduce risks at work (ch. III, s. I, art. 9). We also observed that companies were required to carry out medical examinations of personnel at the following stages (ch. VI, art. 26):

- at the time of recruitment
- at regular intervals during course of employment
- at the stage of exiting the company

Furthermore, the regulations also required employers to train workers and keep them informed about occupational safety, health, and security (ch. III, s. I, art. 11). In addition, all business entities with fifty or more workers were required to set up work accident prevention committees (*comissão de prevenção de acidentes de trabalho* or CPAT), according to ch. IX, art. 33. It was noted in the same legal clause that employers with special cases of exposure of occupational accidents and illnesses were required to form such committees even with a staff of less than fifty workers.

We believed that the legal requirements specified in these regulations were crucial processes for effective management of the risks related to work-related accidents and occupational illnesses. We believed that these measures had the potential to provide practical support in prevention of accidents. However, it was necessary ensure that the employers would actually implement them appropriately. We noted that the regulatory authorities had also established the respective sanctions. The regulations stipulated that a fine of up to ten times the average salary of the company would be applied for each contravention (ch. VIII, art. 31). We believed that this regulatory framework could be used as the basis for risk surveys by the insurance companies. We also believed that entities such as the Insurance Association could play a role on developing guidelines regarding some of the critical legal conditions, such as the requirement for internal regulations on occupational safety, hygiene, and health (ch. III, s. I, art. 9, item e).

## Which entities were supposed to supervise the handling of WCA insurance?

From our review of the WCA insurance regulations, we noted that this class of insurance was subject to supervision and legal reporting conditions to seven different sets of authorities with the following responsibilities:

1. **The insurance regulator** within the Ministry of Finance was responsible for all insurance activities, as reinforced in the WCA insurance regulations (ch. XIII, art. 58).
2. **The Ministry of Labour** had authority to monitor compliance and apply sanctions for any transgressions (ch. X, art. 47).
3. **The social security authorities** played a critical role in WCA Insurance, and insurers were also required to send defined reports to them (ch. IV, art. 8, cl. 8).

4. Insurers were required to submit to **appropriate courts** specified reports in respect of different forms of claims, as outlined in Appendix IV.

5. **The Ministry of Health** was also supposed to receive obligatory reports from insurers in respect of occupational illness cases (ch. V, art. 15). A representative from the ministry was supposed to preside over deliberations of the body responsible for assessment of disabilities, as discussed below (ch. VII, art. 21, cl. 2).

6. **The National Commission for Assessment of Occupational Disabilities** (Comissão Nacional de Avaliação de Incapacidades Laborais or CNAIL) was responsible for assessing and determining the rates of disability for WCA Insurance on the basis of the National Disability Table (Tabela Nacional de Incapacidade or TNI; ch. X, art. 45).

7. **The Fund for Actualisation of Pensions of Workmen's Accident and Occupational Illnesses** (Fundo de Actualização das Pensões de Acidentes de Trabalho e Doenças Profissionais or FUNDAP) was responsible for reviewing and updating WCA pension claims (ch. VIII, art. 42) and setting up technical reserves (ch. VIII, art. 35, cl. 6).

We understood the important role of all entities included in this list. However, we were of the opinion that Angolan policymakers could take advantage of the planned reform of the insurance regulatory framework to streamline reporting requirements in this area and others, as discussed in this book. In addition, we believed that after submission of required reports by insurers, it would be beneficial for the market if the concerned authorities could process the data and publish appropriate reports to support market development initiatives and inform key stakeholders of major issues arising. In the period of preparing this case study in 2018, we were aware that at least the Ministry of Labour produced a half-yearly report on claims from this class of business. In its report for the first half-year of 2018, it was reported by the inspector-general of labour, Nzinga do Céu, that there were 666 cases of WCA claims, including 278 major injuries and nine fatalities (Novo Jornal, 2018c).

Finally, we would like to conclude by indicating that it was not our intention to discuss in this book all the details of WCA Insurance. However, we believed that there were number of critical issues with this type of insurance business. In our review of the same type of risk in Mozambique, we also identified many challenges with the risk management, insurance underwriting, reserving, accounting, claims management, and respective reinsurance. In addition, WCA insurance policies tended to have a long tail of exposure, as well as some form of uncapped liability that could pose risks of lack of financial soundness. This problem was likely to become more prominent given plans by regulators in Angola and other African markets to adopt an emerging-risk-based regulatory framework. This approach placed more emphasis than traditional compliance-based models of regulation on the need for insurers to identify, assess, and control the risks to which they are exposed.

# 7.2 MOTOR THIRD-PARTY LIABILITY INSURANCE

The Highway Code of Angola, enacted in the decree-law no. 5/08 of 29 September 2008, established part of the legal basis for obligatory insurance for motor third-party liability and for motor sports (ch. I, s. IV, art. 129 to 131). Furthermore, in the Basic Law of Land Transport (*Lei de Bases dos Transportes Terrestres*), as provided for in law no. 20, 03 of 19 August 2003, 'Third Party Insurance' (*Seguro contra Terceiros*) was obligatory for all land-transport vehicles (ch. I, art. 10). This insurance was obligatory for both private and public transportation activities in the national territory of Angola, and cover was supposed to include passengers and goods (ch. I, art. 3).

Further to the two legal references to obligatory insurance for motor vehicles, we noted that the minister of finance established a technical committee to prepare draft legislation regarding obligatory motor third-party liability insurance (*seguro obrigatório de responsabilidade civil automóvel*) as per decree no. 116/05 of 1 July 2006. The committee included representatives of ENSA and AAA Seguros as well as members from the insurance supervisory body and other concerned government authorities. This committee executed the required work following the regulations of the

Insurance Technical Council (CTSF). We discussed this entity in Chapter 3. Following completion of the task of this committee, regulations on motor third-party liability were approved in decree no. 35/09 of 11 August 2009. The key features of this obligatory insurance are outlined below.

## Which vehicles were required to have motor third-party liability insurance?

All categories of vehicles, including bicycles, were required to have motor third-party liability insurance for both material damage and bodily injury (ch. I, art. 2, cl. 1). Locomotives were also required to have this obligatory third-party cover (ch. I, art. 2, cl. 2). The same obligatory cover was also required for agricultural vehicles driven on public roads (ch. I, art. 2, cl. 2). Only vehicles belonging to organs of the state were exempt from this obligatory motor liability insurance (ch. I, art. 4, cl. 2). It was the normal practice in most other African markets for the insurance markets to exempt the state from obligatory insurance, and in most instances, government property, in general, was completely uninsured. However, even though the state could use the law to make itself exempt from placing insurance with the private insurance market, we believed that it would be an example of good governance if it were to consider setting up formal risk-control mechanisms.

## What was the geographic scope of the obligatory motor third-party liability insurance?

As per regulations, the obligatory cover had territorial scope of the whole of Angola. As a result of this requirement, all insurers underwriting this policy were supposed to ensure that they had representation in all provincial cities through branches, correspondents and/or agents (ch. I, art. 5). Furthermore, foreign registered vehicles entering Angola were required to buy obligatory motor liability insurance at the border unless they had the Yellow Card Insurance, for which the Insurance Association of Angola was supposed to serve as the national bureau.

Notwithstanding the existence of clear rules and regulations on Motor Third Party Liability insurance and respective guidelines, the majority of vehicles on the road remained uninsured. Key stakeholders in the insurance market put much of the blame on the national police, who were accused of not enforcing this obligatory type of insurance. On the part of the police, they argued that they needed training and guidance on this compulsory insurance and appropriate tools to do their work (Silva, 2018). We observed similar issues of failure to enforce this type of insurance in Mozambique (Muchena, 2018: 170).

## Were there guidelines and standard obligatory policy wordings for compulsory motor third-party liability insurance?

We observed that besides the WCA insurance, motor third-party liability was one of the types of insurance where there was a detailed guideline on how risk was supposed to be underwritten. The Guidelines on Insurance Rating Systems, as provided for in executive decree no. 58/02 of 5 December 2002, stipulated the approved standard insurance market premium rates (art. 13). Insurance companies were required to adopt and implement these fixed rates in their underwriting (art. 1, cl. 2a). The insurance market was also supposed to issue only the standard policy wording (*apólice uniforme*), as part of the rules stipulated in the Insurance Contract Regulations (ch. V, art. 52).

## Was Angola covered by the Yellow Card system?

The motor third-party liability regulations discussed above referred only to liability within Angola. We could not establish if there were separate regulations applicable for land transportation outside of Angola to neighbouring countries. We were aware that Angola did not have access to the COMESA Yellow Card Insurance System[31] covering some of the key neighbouring countries of Angola in the east and the north. However, it appeared that Angola was invited to join the scheme and had been participating as an observer in some of the meetings of this initiative from the 1980s (Nazaré, 2008: 103).

---

[31] The COMESA Yellow Card System was a regional motor third-party liability insurance for vehicles in transit in the covered member states of the COMESA regional grouping: http://ycmis.comesa.int/ (accessed: 16/05/2018).

## How was the national motor data centre supposed to operate?

According to the motor third-party liability regulations, appropriate entities in the Home Affairs Ministry, in collaboration with the National Directorate of Road Transport and the Insurance Association (ASAN), were supposed to form a national data centre (*centro de dados*) for the benefit of this class of insurance (ch. V, art. 34). It also specified, in the same section of the law, that this centre was supposed to be set up with financial support of the insurance companies. We could not trace any other directive that explained how insurers were to support the centre. It appeared that there was still a need for the centre to be set up.

# 7.3 AVIATION THIRD-PARTY LIABILITY INSURANCE

As we saw in Chapter 4, the state directly intervened to guarantee insurance cover for the national airline when there were issues of restrictions of cover from the international aviation insurance market. With the exception of cases where the government was compelled to intervene, the Angola commercial insurance market had access to reinsurance for the purposes of covering the obligatory aviation third-party insurance specified in Angolan Civil Aviation Law (*Lei da Aviação Civil*) and respective regulations. The Civil Aviation Law, as enacted in law no. 1/08 of 16 January 2008, stated that third-party liability insurance was required for operators in this sector, including entities providing air transportation, aviation service providers, operators of aviation infrastructure, and ground assistance services (ch. 10, art. 114 and 115).

The regulations in respect of obligatory aviation liability insurance (*seguro obrigatório de responsabilidade civil de aviação*) were laid out in presidential decree no. 226/16 of 17 November 2016. As noted in these regulations, the limits of this obligatory liability insurance would be defined in specific legislation to be issued by the Ministry of Finance (ch. III, Art. 17). Furthermore, the lawmakers provided the following reminders in the same regulatory legislation (ch. III, Art. 18):

- This obligatory aviation liability insurance was subject to obligatory coinsurance, as defined in the regulations on reinsurance and coinsurance discussed in Chapter 8.
- Given that this type of aviation insurance was not part of the registered tariff system, insurers were supposed to submit terms and conditions for review by the insurance regulator.
- Brokerage was prohibited on this type of insurance as per the regulations regarding types of risks subject to obligatory co-insurance.

# 7.4 ENVIRONMENT-RELATED INSURANCE AND GUARANTEES

We observed that there were also requirements in Angola for obligatory forms of insurance or guarantees for environment-related risks. Part of these requirements were on the basis of international conventions on oil pollution, as we shall discuss below. There were also requirements for environmental liabilities arising from the regulatory framework for mining activities as well as all other projects where there was a risk of affecting the environment and for which environmental impact assessments were required.

## Was Angola a member of the International Conventions on Civil Liability for Oil Pollution Damage?

We noted that Angola adopted the International Convention on Civil Liability for Oil Pollution Damage[32] as per resolution no. 32/01 of 1 November 2001. This convention was part of the international legal framework established by the International Maritime Organization (IMO). Angola had been a member state of this specialist agency of the United Nations since 1977.[33] According to this treaty, ships with a capacity of more than 2,000 tons of oil cargo were required to have 'insurance or other financial security' for liability arising from an oil spill. This requirement

---

[32] Referred to in brief as the CLC Convention.
[33] As per the list on the website of IMO: http://www.imo.org/en/About/Membership/Pages/MemberStates.aspx (accessed on 25/06/2018).

could also be relevant for Angola if any of the ships transporting Angolan oil carried the national flag. Besides the above conventions regarding oil pollution, there also existed a local legal requirement in Angola regarding any activity where there existed a risk of environmental damage, as we shall discuss below.

## What were the legal requirements in respect of environmental impairment liability?

We observed that there was reference to some form of environmental impairment liability for all activities that were likely to have an adverse impact on the environment, as defined in presidential decree no. 194/11 of 7 July 2011. This decree approved the regulations in respect of liability for environmental damages (*responsabilidade por danos ambientais*). The types of projects and operations that were required to have these obligatory environmental guarantees and liability policies were as outlined in the regulations on environmental impact assessment (*avaliação de impacto ambiental*), as defined in decree no. 51/04 of 23 July 2004.

Furthermore, the regulations on liability for environmental damages contained, amongst other concepts, the 'Principle of Prevention' (*Princípio de Prevenção*) of damage to the environment and 'Principle of Accountability' (*Princípio da Responsabilização*) for operators responsible for harming the environment (ch. 1, art. 2). In accordance with this decree, all entities pursuing activities that posed a risk of damage to the environment were supposed to set up 'obligatory financial guarantees' (*garantias financeiras obrigatórias*). These environmental guarantees were supposed to be in the form of either insurance guarantees or bank guarantees (ch. IV, art. 20, cl. 2). We could not find any other legislation specifying minimum amounts of cover and specification of the required terms and conditions for such guarantees. We believed that this was an issue that could be addressed in the insurance regulatory framework.

In addition to the obligatory financial environmental guarantees referred to above, the concerned entities were also required to have environmental impairment liability insurance (ch. IV, art. 21). The regulations did not specify the required minimum amount of cover. They only stated that the minimum limits of cover were supposed to represent the average value of costs of environmental damage, repairs, and prevention of damage (ch. IV, art. 22, cl. 4). Besides the environmental damages liability regulations referred to above, we also noted that the new Private Investments Law no. 10/18 of 26 June 2018 also stated that private investors were required to insure for, amongst other things, environmental liability (ch. IV, art. 18, item h). We could not trace any regulations on the nature of insurance policies required. We were aware that the existing insurance market had underwriting capacity for environmental damage arising from only 'sudden, unintended and unforeseen occurrence', as defined in conventional liability policies. Such policies did not cover damage caused by gradual seepage, pollution, or contamination. We believed that there was a need for the insurance regulatory framework to assist with appropriate guidelines on the coverage of environmental liability.

## What were the obligatory types of insurance for mining activities?

The Mining Code (*Código Mineiro*) of Angola, as provided for in law no. 31/11 of 23 September 2011, also made reference to compulsory forms of insurance for mining activities. We noted that the technical management of mines could be held personally responsible for civil and criminal liability to the Angolan state and to third parties (ch. VIII, s. III, sub-s. III, art.145). The law specified that all industrial mining operations were required to have 'all risks insurance' (*seguro contra todos os riscos*) covering the following (ch. VIII, s. III, sub-s. III, art. 153):
- property damage of mining installations
- third-party liability
- work-related accidents of mining personnel

It appeared that there were no regulations defining the terms and conditions of the required property damage and third-party liability insurance. At least the work-related accidents were fairly well regulated under the WCA insurance regulations.

## What were the types of obligatory bonds required for mines?

Besides the obligatory insurance of mines, the Mining Code also specified two forms of obligatory guarantees. First, the code stated that private mining companies were required to have performance guarantee bonds (part I, vol. I, ch. IV, s. II, art. 62). The bonds were supposed to be for 2 per cent of the investment value at the prospection, research, and evaluation phase and 4 per cent at the operational stage. It was stated that this bond was supposed to be either a bank guarantee or another form of guarantees accepted by law. Second, the Mining Code referred to mining rehabilitation bonds that were supposed to be set up in the last year of the operations of a mine (part I, vol. IV, ch. XVI, s. II, sub-s. I, art. 250, cl. 4). This bond was supposed to replace financial provisions for environmental restoration that were required during the life span of the mine. The limits for this financial provision and the subsequent bond were to be in accordance with the limits stipulated in the respective environmental impact assessment report of the mining project.

In the respective legal provisions of the Mining Code, the law referred specifically to bank guarantees or equivalent forms of guarantees. We were aware that, in practice, the authorities in Angola could accept insurance bonds and guarantees as substitutes for bank guarantees. The challenge tended to be that insurance companies lacked the technical and financial underwriting capacity for such types of bonds. We believed that this was a major area of development in Angola as well as other African insurance markets.

We had observed that insurance guarantees had contributed significantly to growth of the insurance market in countries such as Brazil. At the time of writing this book, the financial lines business there, which consisted mainly of bonds, had an annual turnover of more than US$1 billion. This growth of bonds in Brazil was triggered by development of an appropriate legal framework to support underwriting and setting up of appropriate mechanisms to secure the respective risk. We believed that this could be a major growth area in Angola for bonds in mining and all other major economic activities where they were required.

# 7.5 PROFESSION-RELATED OBLIGATORY POLICIES

## What was the form of obligatory professional indemnity insurance required for intermediaries?

As we discussed in Chapter 6, the Regulations of Insurance Intermediaries, decree no. 7/03 of 24 January 2003, stated that professional indemnity insurance was required for intermediaries. Besides the specification of minimum limits of cover ($100,000 for insurance intermediaries and $200,000 for reinsurance brokers), there were no other guidelines on the required obligatory policy. We believed that it would be useful for the authorities to provide more guidance on the nature and scope of cover. Furthermore, the limits of cover could be linked to levels of exposure depending on the size of accounts handled by the intermediary. We believed that the more professional intermediaries would already have appropriate limits of cover. This type of insurance was often presented by the intermediaries as one of the benefits of protection that could be enjoyed by clients who chose to work with them. From some of the major projects in southern Africa, we noted that the standard amount of professional indemnity insurance that was required was at least US$10 million.

## What was the obligatory type of insurance for travel agents?

There was a legal requirement for an obligatory insurance to cover liability of travel agents. This legal requirement was defined in decree no. 54/97 of 1 August 1997 containing regulations of the licensing and operations of travel agents. These regulations specified the following two types of obligatory insurance covers:

- First, it was stated in this legislation that it was obligatory for the operator to present a guarantee to cover their activities (ch. IV, art. 27). Guarantees were one of the few financial products that could be obtained from either a banking institution or an insurance company. According to these regulations, it was acceptable to present a guarantee from either an insurer or a bank as long as the issuing entity was registered in Angola (ch. IV, s. I, art. 28)
- Second, it was obligatory for the operators to have a valid travel operators liability insurance (ch. IV, s. II, art. 35 – 37). It was

not clear to us what exactly was the nature of required cover. The regulations named the required type of cover as professional indemnity insurance (*responsabilidade civil profissional*). However, the scope of coverage defined in the same section of the regulations referred to insurance for protection against legal liability for property damage and injury suffered by third parties. This scope of coverage appeared to be referring to types of events that would be covered under public-liability type policies and not professional indemnity.

We would like to note that there was no reference to obligatory insurance for travel operators in the insurance legal framework. As part of the planned reform process of the legislation of insurance, there could be improved guidelines as well as updated limits of cover for these types of insurance that were supposed to be obligatory.

## What was the required form of insurance cover for freight forwarders?

According to decree no. 68/89 relating to freight forwarding activities,[34] licensed operators in this activity were required to have liability insurance. The scope of coverage for this obligatory insurance was defined in the following regulations (ch. II, art. 12). We observed that the subsequent regulations (executive Decree no. 9/90 of 31 March 1990) did not provide the required definition of this insurance. We should note that it was not uncommon to make this insurance obligatory; such was the case in a Portuguese law, decree-law no. 255/99 of 7 July 1999, which specified the nature of liability covered as well as minimum limit of liability.

## What form of liability insurance was obligatory for health professionals?

There was reference to an obligatory insurance in the National Health System law no. 21-B/92 of 28 August 1992. It was stated in this law that health professionals were supposed to have insurance cover against risks arising from the practice of their profession as a private business (ch. IX, art. 35, cl. 4). There was no definition of the exact type of obligatory

---

[34] Referred to in the law in Portuguese as *actividade transitária*

insurance and the respective required limits of cover. We were aware that in developed markets, medical malpractice insurance was one of the key types of policies that was a critical requirement for the health sector. However, we were also aware that most insurers on the African continent avoided this class of insurance, since reinsurance markets, in general, were reluctant to underwrite this form of liability due to past claims experience.

### What type of insurance policy was required for sportspersons?

There was reference to an obligatory type of insurance for sportspersons in the law of the sporting system of Angola, as defined in law no. 10/98 of 9 October 1998. It was stated in this law that in order to protect sportspersons from risks inherent in their sporting activities, there was supposed to be an obligatory insurance scheme (ch. II, s. I, art. 5, cl. 2). It was not clear which types of insurance policies were being referred to.

According to references in earlier legislation to this type of insurance, it appeared that the required insurance was personal accident (Nazaré, 2008: 104). However, traditional insurance markets, such as the one in Angola, had capacity only for personal accident policies excluding sports and other high-risk activities. We were aware that in specialist markets like Lloyds, it was possible to obtain this type of insurance. We knew that some of the top Angolan sportspersons in international markets probably had access to such types of cover. That was not likely to be the case for the majority of amateur and professional sportspersons based in Angola.

## 7.6 OTHER TYPES OF OBLIGATORY PRIVATE INSURANCE

### What type of insurance was required for public companies by law?

According to the public companies law no. 9/95 of 15 September 1995, public companies were required to insure their property. It was stated in the same law that the economic and financial minister would determine which types of goods required obligatory insurance (ch. III, s. III, art. 26, cl. 2). In the respective regulations of this law, as per decree no. 8/02 published on 29 April 2002, there was no reference to insurance. As noted by de Abreu (2014: 438), besides property insurance, a public company also required other essential types of insurance. This Angolan insurance writer was of the opinion that there was also a need for general liability[35] to insure against damage to third parties and to the environment. We would like to add that for public companies, it was also important to consider making it compulsory for them to have directors and officers liability insurance.

## What were the types of obligatory insurance required for construction projects?

The law regarding construction, as provided for in decree no. 80/06 of 30 October 2006, also referred to two types of required insurance. All applications for construction licences were supposed to have, amongst other legal requirements, the following types of insurance:
- policy to compensate for work-related accidents (ch. II, s. V, art. 50, cl. 1b)
- construction insurance policy (ch. II, s. V, art. 50, cl. 2).

We were aware that the requirement regarding work-related accidents was supposed to be covered by WCA insurance, as discussed at the beginning of this chapter. For the requirement regarding a construction insurance policy, we did not locate any other regulations specifying the limits, nature, and scope of required insurance cover.

## What were the types of obligatory insurance specified in the regulations regarding port concessions?

There was reference to a requirement for insurance in the legislation pertaining to operators in port concessions. According to the port concessions decree no. 52/97 of 18 July 1997, concessionaires required insurance to protect them against risks arising from their business activity (s. XIII, art. 51, cl. 1). It was stated in the same clause that such insurance included material damage cover and liability for work-related accidents and personal injuries of any nature. Although there was no specific definition of the types of required insurance, at least in the second clause of the same

---

[35] . This was our translation for the expression *'responsabilidade civil exploração'*, as used by the author.

article, it was also stated that customs of the industry were supposed to be followed in arranging such insurance cover. According to de Abreu (2014: 439), at least in this particular case there was reference to the requirement for liability insurance besides insurance of property, as per the law relating to insurance of public companies.

## What were the obligatory insurances required for non-governmental organisations?

We were also able to review the current legislation in respect of activities of non-governmental organisations (NGOs) as provided for in decree no. 74/15 of 23 March 2015 (*governo de Angola*). These regulations referred to, amongst other legal obligations, two forms of compulsory insurance (ch. V, art. 23, cl.1q). The regulations referred to work accident insurance (*acidentes de trabalho*), for which there were appropriate rules and regulations as per the WCA insurance regulatory framework, as discussed above. However, there was also reference to a legal requirement for specifically public liability insurance (*seguros de responsabilidade civil*) for NGOs. There appeared not to be any further legislation clarifying the exact type of insurance and respective minimum amounts of cover, as was the norm for obligatory types of insurance.

# 7.7 FUTURE DEVELOPMENTS

We noted that there were still a number of challenges to be addressed in this category of insurance. One of the key issues affecting especially motor third-party liability insurance was the lack of compliance by the people and entities that were expected to insure as required by law. We believed that it would be useful for Angola and the rest of the African markets for appropriate entities to conduct a case study aimed at identifying models that had been most successful at ensuring compliance. We noted that there tended to be a high penetration rate when this type of insurance was embedded in another critical service that target consumers were already buying in large volumes. It tended to be useful if the product or service in question already had existing distribution channels.

In addition, we noted that for WCA insurance, there were numerous reporting requirements to different authorities besides the insurance regulator. We had also seen that this type of insurance could be given critical support through existing legislation aimed at promoting a culture of good risk management. The key challenge at the moment was a lack of implementation and enforcement. We were also concerned about the lack of mechanisms to protect the interests of beneficiaries of pension claims from this type of product. We believed that, at best, there was supposed to be an autonomous fund to protect and preserve these pensions.

Besides the regulated compulsory types of insurance, there were also numerous types of supposedly obligatory insurance policies and insurance guarantees that were not regulated. We were also aware that there were current consultation processes on a new draft law for obligatory marine cargo insurance (AngoNotícias, 2018). As reported in the same article, the insurance regulator viewed the process of making this type of insurance obligatory as a key step in promoting growth and development of the insurance market. If this law was passed and this insurance implemented, it would be a major line of business, as Angola depended on a significant amount of importations of capital goods, plant machinery, equipment, medicines, textiles, and food.

# References

Achega, Gonçalo. (2014). ***Legislação de Mercados Financeiros, Direito Bancário e dos Seguros***. Luanda – Plural Editores.

AngoNotícias (2018), 'Seguros: Regulador diz que não há risco de falência', as published on 14/04/2018 at http://www.angonoticias.com/Artigos/item/57664/seguros-regulador-diz-que-nao-ha-risco-de-falencia.

AXCO (2011), *Angola: Non-Life Insurance Market Report*. London: AXCO Insurance Information Services.

de Abreu, Ana Edith Viegas, (2014), *100 Anos de Legislação de Seguros em Angola*. Luanda: Edições Chá de Caxinde.

Demirgüç-Kunt, Asli, Baybars Karacaovali, and Luc Laeven (2005). 'Deposit Insurance around the World: A Comprehensive Database," World Bank website, http://siteresources.worldbank.org/INTRES/Resources/469232-1107449512766/DepositInsuranceDatabasePaper_DKL.pdf (accessed 16 April 2018).

Governo de Angola. *Regulamento das Organizações Não Governamentais*. [Accessed 15 May 2018] http://www.governo.gov.ao/VerLegislacao.aspx?id=777

International Maritime Organization (2018). International Convention on Civil Liability for Oil Pollution Damage http://www.imo.org/en/About/conventions/listofconventions/pages/international-convention-on-civil-liability-for-oil-pollution-damage-(clc).aspx

Muchena, Israel (2018), *Development of Insurance in Mozambique*. Bloomington: AuthorHouse.

Nazaré, Domingas Miguel (2008), *A ENSA e a Reforma do Sector Seguradora em Angola*. Luanda–Caxinde: Editora e Livraria.

Novo Jornal (2018), '*Nove mortes em 666 acidentes de trabalho registados em Angola no primeiro semestre de 2018*', http://www.novojornal.co.ao/sociedade/

interior/nove-mortes-em-666-acidentes-de-trabalho-registados-em-angola-no-primeiro-semestre-de-2018-57140.html?utm_term=Bom+dia%2C+sim.+-+Newsletter+Novo+Jornal&utm_campaign=Newsletters&utm_source=e-goi&utm_medium=email (accessed on 1 August 2018).

Silva, Victor (2018), 'Fundo de Garantia Automóvel Angolano é um Fiasco', *Jornal de Angola,* http://jornaldeangola.sapo.ao/opiniao/fundo_de_garantia_automovel__angolano_e_um_fiasco (accessed 18 May 2018).

# Chapter 8

# COINSURANCE AND REINSURANCE

In the post-independence period in most insurance markets on the African continent, one of the key goals of policymakers was to implement policies aimed at promoting local retention of insured risks. In studies conducted by the United Nations Conference on Trade and Development (UNCTAD) in the 1970s on the deficits in the balance of payments of developing countries, it was observed that one of the areas of high 'outflows' of foreign exchange was the purchase of insurance and reinsurance abroad (Irukwu, 1998: 206).

In order to address this identified problem, UNCTAD promoted policies of formation of national and regional reinsurance companies, along with other measures aimed at increasing retention of the local insurance market. As we discussed in Chapter 3, in the post-independence period, Angola had created a monopoly insurance and reinsurance company known as ENSA. Following the ending of the monopoly market in 2000, Angolan policymakers introduced new regulations intended to support development of local underwriting capacity and retention of risk in the emerging competition-based market. As we shall discuss below, the policies that were initiated were an obligatory coinsurance scheme and establishment.

## 8.1 OBLIGATORY COINSURANCE

We should begin by explaining that coinsurance was a normal process used by insurers to share risks in Angolan and most other insurance markets in Africa and worldwide. Coinsurance was seen as one of the mechanisms of boosting local retention of risks before risks were transferred into reinsurance markets. In most African markets, this process of sharing risks amongst local insurers was a voluntary process. Due to a realization that competing insurers would not always be willing to share information and collaborate on major risks, the Angolan authorities chose to implement a policy of obligatory coinsurance, as we shall discuss below.

## Which types of insurance were subject to obligatory coinsurance?

Both the principal General Law of Insurance and the reinsurance and coinsurance regulations contained references to obligatory coinsurance. The General Law of Insurance stated that public insurers were to underwrite insurance policies of central organs of the state and then to coinsure this business with the rest of the licensed insurers in the market (ch. IV, art. 40, cl. 2). Furthermore, the Council of Ministers had the authority to determine other special types of insurance to be insured by public insurers and for which coinsurance, with the rest of the insurers in the market, would be required (ch. IV, art. 40, cl. 4). In the reinsurance and coinsurance regulations, as provided for in decree no. 6/ 01 of 2 March 2001 (ch. III, art. 16), it was stated that the following types of insurance were also subject to obligatory coinsurance:
- oil and gas sector
- diamond mining
- public sector aviation
- agriculture

Furthermore, as stipulated in the same regulations, coinsurance for these businesses was not supposed to be for less than 30 per cent of the insured risk (ch. III, art. 16, cl. 3). The coinsurance leader had the exclusive responsibility to arrange any foreign reinsurance that would be required on this obligatory coinsurance business (ch. III, art. 16, cl. 5).

## What were the allocations of coinsurance shares amongst the registered insurers?

The reinsurance and coinsurance regulations did not provide a breakdown of the allocations for coinsurance business amongst the registered operators. We were able to trace references to the allocations in some of the documents issued by the Minister of Finance confirming authorisation to new insurance companies in the period 2004 to 2007 as follows:

- decree no. 24/04 of 7 September 2004 authorizing establishment of NOSSA Seguros, SA
- decree no. 360/05 of 21 October 2005 authorizing establishment of A Mundial Seguros, SA
- decree no. 7/05 of 21 January 2005 authorising the establishment GA Seguros, SA
- decree no. 185/07 of 14 February 2007 authorizing the establishment of Garantia Seguros, SA

In the post-independence phase, 2004 was a critical turning point, since the authorization of NOSSA Seguros marked the beginning of re-entry of privately owned insurance companies since the formation of the two public insurance companies—ENSA and AAA Seguros. In view of this change, we observed that the decree of authorization of NOSSA (no. 204/04 of 7 September 2004) also contained rules regarding how new insurers were to collaborate with the existing public insurers in the obligatory coinsurance. In this decree, an allocation of 10 per cent was granted to NOSSA (art. 3) and the balance reallocated to the existing insurers (art. 4). With the references from this decree and the others up to 2007, we noted that the coinsurance shares of the expanding number of insurers were allocated as presented in Table 8.

## Table 8: Coinsurance Share Allocations Up to 2007

| Insurer | Decree | Up to 7 Sept. 2004 | After 7 Sept. 2004 | 21 Jan. 2005 | 3 Jun. 2005 | 21 Oct. 2005 | 14 Feb. 2007 |
|---|---|---|---|---|---|---|---|
| ENSA | 204/ 04 of 7 Sept. | 55.00% | 49.50% | 44.00% | 44.00% | 37.40% | 29.70% |
| AAA | | 45.00% | 40.50% | 36.00% | 36.00% | 30.60% | 24.30% |
| NOSSA | | n.a. | 10.00% | 10.00% | 10.00% | 8.00% | 8.00% |
| GA Seguros | 7/05 of 21 Jan. | n.a. | n.a. | 10.00% | 10.00% | 8.00% | 8.00% |
| Global | 87/05 of 3 Jun. | n.a. | n.a. | n.a. | 10.00% | 8.00% | 8.00% |

| A Mundial | 360/05 of 21 Oct. | n.a. | n.a. | n.a. | n.a. | 8.00% | 8.00% |
|---|---|---|---|---|---|---|---|
| Garantia | 185/07 of 14 Feb. | n.a. | n.a. | n.a. | n.a. | n.a. | 8.00% |
| **Total** | | **100.00%** | **100.00%** | **100.00%** | **110.00%** | **100.00%** | **100.00%** |

From our review of the allocations of coinsurance shares by the insurance regulator in the period from 2004 to 2007, we noted that there might have been an over-allocation in the decree of 3 June 2005. The coinsurance shares referred to in this regulatory document were for more than 100 per cent.

Furthermore, we observed that from 2008 to date, the regulator no longer automatically allocated coinsurance shares to new companies. As we had already noted, the decrees for companies registered from this date on stated that they could only qualify for obligatory coinsurance after publishing of the first year of financial results and demonstrating appropriate levels of financial soundness. We could not trace any other legal instrument that could allow us to follow the reallocations to date. From discussions at activities like the annual Oil and Gas Forum in Luanda, we knew that a number of registered insurers were not satisfied with the lack of transparency on how the coinsurance business was managed (Hossi, 2018).

## What was the main reason for obligatory coinsurance of certain types of business?

According to the reinsurance and coinsurance regulations, the reason for making certain types of business subject to obligatory coinsurance was to ensure a balanced and harmonious development of the insurance market (ch. III, art. 16, cl. 1). We were aware that the intention of the regulator was to ensure even development of the market. However, it also appeared to us that this policy could have unintended consequences. There existed the risk of attracting to the insurance business many new operators, including investors that were relying mainly on the fact they could secure income through obligatory coinsurance, regardless of the soundness of their business plans and their knowledge of the insurance business. That situation would tend to promote a culture of 'rent seeking' as opposed to a healthy business environment.

Furthermore, we noted that the same regulations stipulated that the leader and following coinsurance companies were supposed to ensure that they satisfied conditions and requirements for solvency as defined in the insurance legal framework (ch. III, art. 16, cl. 6). In our view, this was a critical precondition that could lead to disqualification of many licensed operators. It was also a crucial factor that influenced the low levels of local retention for businesses like oil and gas that had very high exposures. We also noted that Nuno Matos, an actuarial consultant from PwC, raised some of these concerns in his interview with the Angolan newspaper, Expansão (Hebo, 2018: 18). He believed that the majority of the insurance companies in Angola that were supposed to share in the oil and gas risks lacked both the financial capacity and the technical skills to manage such risks. He further argued that, in fact, the insurance regulator was supposed to prevent the companies in question from underwriting such types of risk.

## 8.2 REINSURANCE OF OBLIGATORY COINSURANCE

How was the reinsurance of the obligatory coinsurance business supposed to be handled?

There appeared not to be specific guidelines regarding the handling of reinsurance in the types of business subject to obligatory coinsurance. However, we noted that in the annex to the decree in respect of authorization of NOSSA, there were some notes that appeared to address this question. It was clarified that the specified shares of allocation were supposed to apply in the same proportions for both the actual insurance policy and the respective reinsurance of the risks in question. In our view, that approach to reinsurance was part of what was traditionally defined as reinsurance on 'common account basis.'

## What was the procedure to be followed by a new insurer in order to qualify for the obligatory coinsurance business?

We found reference to the procedure to be followed by new insurers in executive decree no. 74/07 of 29 June 2007, providing the Regulations to Streamline the Current Conditions for Accessing and Operating in the Insurance Market. These regulations specified that new insurers only qualified to participate in the obligatory coinsurance business after one year of doing business and following submission of full annual accounts demonstrating that they met the statutory solvency requirements in Angola (art. 2, cl. 1). We had noted that while the licenses granted from 2004 to 2007 automatically allocated obligatory coinsurance shares to new companies, after the passing of this guideline, all the new registrations from 2008 to date referred to this requirement. The new licenses did not automatically qualify for allocations of the obligatory coinsurance.

Moreover, we noted from the above regulations that, after clearance of this first set of accounts, the insurance regulator was supposed to send to the lead coinsurer a declaration authorising the new insurer to participate in the coinsurance scheme (art. 2, cl. 2). We were not able to determine which of the registered insurers had received clearance to participate in this business. We were also aware that a number of registered insurers had not been able to publish audited annual accounts without any qualifications.

# 8.3 LEADERSHIP OF THE OBLIGATORY COINSURANCE

## Which insurer was the leader for the national oil and gas insurance portfolio?

AAA Seguros served as the leading insurer for the oil and gas business from the early days of its establishment in 2001 up to 2016. The leadership position of the obligatory coinsurance business was shifted to ENSA following the passing of presidential order no. 39/16 of 30 March 2016. From our research, we also found reference to this change of leadership in the published accounts of AAA Reinsurance Ltd on the website of the Bermuda Monetary Authority (2017: 7). It was noted that the financial position of this captive insurer related to AAA Seguros was affected by the fact that there was no new business from 2016. From our review of the income statement in the same accounts, we noted that premium income was reduced by 36 per cent from US$413.2 million to US$263.3 million. It was noted that this license would be placed into run-off with effect from 10 November 2016. We should also note that according to the balance sheet of the same entity, the total assets of the company were more than US$.5 billion.

According to the presidential order of 30 March 2016, the insurance regulator was supposed to present to the minister of finance within six months an in-depth study of a new model for coinsurance and reinsurance of the oil and gas sector (art. 7). More than two years after the passing of this legislation, it was not clear if the insurance regulator had presented the required study. At the time of preparing to publish this book, we were aware that the rest of the insurance companies were still waiting for a confirmation of the new model and allocation of shares amongst all the local insurers that qualified for this business.

Furthermore, we were aware that some of the key market observers, such as Nuno Matos from PwC, had concerns about the financial and technical capacity of most of the licensed insurers to underwrite and manage oil and gas risks (Hebo, 2018: 18). However, the lack of progress in the national policy of sharing of oil and gas business had not discouraged most of the local insurance market. Some of the insurers continued to prepare themselves for this business and arranging seminars for skills development and presentation of models for underwriting of such risks from other oil and gas producer countries.

## What were the functions of the coinsurance leader?

The reinsurance and coinsurance regulations specified the functions of the coinsurance leader as follows (ch. III, art. 15):

a) Receive the insurance proposal from the policyholder, analyse the risk, and set the respective terms and conditions of insurance.

b) Issue the insurance policy, collect the premium, and settle any claims.

c) Propose or accept the cancellation of the contract of insurance.

d) Execute actions laid down in law in the event of failure to pay a premium or an instalment of a premium that was due.

e) Any other functions as agreed by the coinsurers.

We should highlight that the regulations stated that the leader was legally liable to the following coinsurers for losses or damages arising as a result of failing to execute the functions noted above and any other tasks agreed upon in the respective coinsurance agreement (ch. III, art. 15, cl. 8).

During the second edition of the Oil and Gas Forum in Luanda in June 2018, there was some debate on the current model for coinsurance. According to some of the key stakeholders, the current situation—where there was only one leader handling all the underwriting—was not the ideal model to support development of local skills and sharing of technical know-how with the rest of the following insurers (Hossi, 2018).

## How were claim settlements supposed to be handled on a coinsured policy?

As per the legal provisions of the reinsurance and coinsurance regulations, claims occurring on a coinsured policy could be settled on the basis of either of the two options noted below (Ch. III, art. 15, cl. 6):

- The coinsurance leader could settle the full amount of the claim on its behalf and on behalf of the coinsurers on their account,
- Each coinsurer could settle directly to the insured their respective share of risk.

## What was the underwriting capacity of the Angola insurance market for the key types of business targeted for local retention?

Following our review of obligatory coinsurance in Angola, it was crucial to get an understanding of the actual financial underwriting capacity of the local insurance market. The capacity of the Angolan insurance market consisted of conventional reinsurance treaties that excluded the oil and gas business. In other words, the local insurance market lacked financial underwriting capacity to retain any meaningful portion of the risks subject to obligatory coinsurance and local retention.

We were aware that it was not only Angola where the local insurance markets were not able to provide required underwriting and financial capacity to meet the aggressive local retention requirements of the policymakers. We believed that regional bodies, such as the African

Insurance Organisation, could commission a study on some of the best practices for an effective strategy of development of local retention policy for oil and gas risks. We would also recommend that, as part of the key objectives of the study, it would need to actually obtain and present practical guidelines and articles of association for some of the best case studies. We believed that among some of the newer oil and gas producing countries, Uganda could have developed one of the more sustainable approaches through the concept of a national oil and gas pool that was actually backed up with specific financial capacity.

Following our review of the rules and regulations in respect of coinsurance, we could see that the current policy framework was aimed at promoting local retention and local content. The policymakers also intended to ensure harmonious development of the insurance market by passing legislation aimed at making it obligatory for all the licensed insurers to share through coinsurance key strategic risks, such as the oil and gas business, which represented the bulk of the current premium income in the market.

# 8.4 REINSURANCE REGULATORY FRAMEWORK

## What was the legal framework for reinsurance in Angola?

The General Law of Insurance was supposed to apply to both insurance and reinsurance (ch. IV, art. 40, cl. 1). All the legal provisions relating to the technical aspects and operations of the insurance business were also intended to cover reinsurance where applicable. Further regulations regarding reinsurance were contained in the same regulations covering the obligatory coinsurance, as per our discussions at the beginning of this chapter. The Reinsurance and Coinsurance Regulations were covered in decree no. 6/01 of 2 March 2001[36] (Dias, 2012: 326–343).

---

[36] Referred to in Portuguese as '*Decreto no. 6/01 de 2 de Março*'.

## Which entities were authorised to reinsure Angolan business?

According to the legal conditions in the Reinsurance and Coinsurance Regulations, only the following five types of entities could reinsure Angolan business (ch. I, art. 2):

1. Reinsurance companies established in Angola, in accordance with the conditions defined in the General Law of Insurance
2. Agencies of international reinsurers set up in Angola as per the conditions to be authorised by the minister of finance and subject to a special registration by the insurance regulator
3. Agencies of international reinsurers in which the Angolan government was a shareholder
4. Licensed insurance companies in Angola
5. Foreign companies authorised in their countries to do reinsurance business

## Could reinsurance be quoted in a foreign currency?

We were aware that most economies in Africa, including Angola, had suffered major problems due the 2016–17 foreign exchange crisis. One of the major challenges that insurers in Angola faced was to avoid foreign exchange losses following depreciation of the local currency. Furthermore, the long waiting periods for clearance of their applications worsened their foreign-exchange loss exposures. As specified in the reinsurance and coinsurance regulations, reinsurance placed abroad could be quoted in the respective foreign currency (ch. I, art. 6).

## Which transactions required clearance by the central bank?

According to the reinsurance and coinsurance regulations (ch. 1, art. 7), reinsurance transactions required prior clearance by the central bank of Angola, Banco Nacional de Angola (BNA), as per the Foreign Exchange Law of Angola. The transactions requiring such clearance included settlement of premium, commission, and claims for reinsurance and retrocession. It was also stated in the reinsurance and coinsurance regulations that the insurance regulator could be required to approve any of the applications for foreign remittances (ch. I, art. 7, cl. 3). In such cases, it was expected that the insurance regulator would provide feedback within time periods defined in the law.

## What were the conditions regarding holding of assets representing reinsurance reserves?

The assets representing technical reinsurance reserves from both local and foreign reinsurers were supposed to be held in Angola as per the rules of the reinsurance and coinsurance regulations (ch. I, art. 8). We were aware that reinsurers tended to avoid the setting up of premiums and loss reserves. Reinsurers avoided leaving reserves in the hands of insurers for understandable reasons. International reinsurers would want to limit investment risk exposures in countries like Angola that had major challenges of foreign exchange volatility and poor sovereign rating that would impair their assets.

# 8.5 NATIONAL REINSURANCE COMPANY

## What was the progress in setting up the proposed national reinsurance company of Angola?

At the time of preparing to publish this book in the last quarter of 2018, the Angolan authorities had been trying to set up a national reinsurance company since the beginning of the twenty-first century. The official process was formalised when the Council of Ministers approved decree no. 2/03 of 10 January 2003 for the establishment of a national reinsurance company, Ango-Re (Sociedade Angolana de Reseguro or SARL). It was supposed to start with paid-up capital of $15 million, and this could be subsequently increased to $50 million. However, the establishment of the company was not completed. Then, through ministerial decree no. 359 of 24 September 2008, a committee of the establishment (*comissão instaladora*) of Ango-Re was set up. The committee was supposed to complete the work of establishment of the new national reinsurer in 120 days.

Unfortunately, the 2008 initiative also failed to complete the work of establishment of the national reinsurer. Following the passage of ministerial decree no. 426/15 of 29 December 2015, another establishment committee was set up. This time, it was a bigger committee consisting of eight members and an even tougher timeline of ninety days to complete the required work of setting up of Ango-Re. It appeared that the authorities were pledging to complete the establishment of the new reinsurer by the end of 2018 (Macauhub: 2018).

# 8.6 OBLIGATORY NATIONAL AND REGIONAL REINSURANCE

We should note that there was not yet any local reinsurer or agency of an international reinsurer established in Angola at the time of writing this book. We believed that when eventually a local reinsurer was going to be set up, it was supposed to benefit from the protection of existing regulations on obligatory local reinsurance as discussed below. In the interim, the local insurance market was not observing the regulations on minimum obligatory reinsurance specified below, since there was not yet a local reinsurer.

## What was the minimum obligatory local reinsurance in Angola?

As provided for in the reinsurance and coinsurance regulations, insurance companies in Angola were required to make an obligatory reinsurance cession of a minimum of 30 per cent to local reinsurers established on the basis of the first three types noted above (ch. I, art. 3). Insurers could reinsure the balance of their business either locally or abroad. The minister of finance had the authority to review the level of obligatory reinsurance.

Furthermore, even when the new national reinsurer was set up, we believed that the local insurance market would still require a significant amount of international reinsurance. Some of the risks for business such as oil and gas had values-at-risk, whereby a share of 30 per cent could represent exposure of more than $1 billion. The new national reinsurer would certainly not have adequate capital, spread of risk, experience, and income base to support local retention of such a level of exposure.

Furthermore, as noted by Swiss Re CEO Christian Mumenthaler in the CEO Risk Forum (2017: 8), effective function of reinsurance was dependent on the following:

- 'freedom of contract, and contract certainty'
- 'international risk transfer and free capital flow'
- capital requirements that reflect a reinsurer's individual risk profile

We were aware that there was an ongoing debate in African and international markets on whether there was supposed to be more protection of local markets or more open markets. In countries like Brazil, the authorities were reducing barriers aimed at protecting the local reinsurance market. At the same time, in countries like India and China, there were increasing restrictions on cross-border reinsurance. Besides the issue of local compulsory reinsurance, we should also review the situation regarding regional reinsurance cessions.

## Were Angolan insurers required to cede obligatory reinsurance to regional reinsurers?

The reinsurance and coinsurance regulations stipulated that any obligatory reinsurance abroad to reinsurers for which Angola could be a member state was considered as part of the total of obligatory reinsurance for Angola (ch. I, art. 3, cl. 4). We were aware that Angola was a shareholder of the African Reinsurance Corporation and had passed legislation in respect of its membership of this regional reinsurer, as provided for in resolution no. 10/91 of 18 May 1991. This resolution provided the approval for the Republic of Angola to join the establishment agreement of the African Reinsurance Corporation (Africa Re). We also noted that for all twenty-one companies registered from 2005 to date, the respective decree (*despacho*) from the minister of finance stipulated that they were supposed to make compulsory cessions to Africa Re in accordance with the establishment agreement of the Africa Re (1976).

However, Angolan lawmakers had not yet passed appropriate legislation to ensure compliance and enforcement of the statutory 5 per cent reinsurance cession to Africa Re as per the requirement specified in the establishment agreement (ch. VI, art. 27, cl. 2). Nonetheless, we noted that most of the insurers in the market tended to place reinsurance business with Africa Re on a voluntary basis. We observed that such voluntary placements with Africa Re were for more than the 5 per cent compulsory for most lines of business, except mainly for the specialist lines of business of aviation, oil, and gas. The local insurance market tended to place these risks predominantly in international reinsurance markets. Besides Africa Re, the other compulsory cession that was applicable in some of the territories in the zone where Angola was located was the statutory reinsurance made to the regional reinsurance company, PTA Reinsurance Company.[37] However, as we discussed in Chapter 1, Angola was not yet a member of COMESA.

## 8.7 CROSS-BORDER REINSURANCE

### Was there a cross-border reinsurance regulatory framework in Angola?

We had not seen any regulations in Angola regarding specifically cross-border reinsurance. This problem was not unique to Angola. As we noted in the review of the *African Insurance Regulation Directory*, very few markets in Africa had specific legal conditions regarding operations of professional reinsurers and their operations. These were 'indirectly supervised through the rules relating to their direct insurance business partners' (Africa Re 2015: 5).

However, in a number of the key economies in the developing world, there were emerging changes on this question. In the past ten years, we saw a number of key emerging markets such as Brazil, China, India, and South Africa starting to develop some forms of cross-border reinsurance regulatory frameworks. Such types of regulations were intended to address issues such as registration and clearance of approved securities as well as definition of maximum levels and types of reinsurance that could be placed with any reinsurance security depending on criteria, including financial credit rating. For some of the major African insurance markets, it could also be useful to see if there could be improvements in this area without creating too

---

[37] More information is available on the website of this company: http://zep-re.com/ (accessed 30 June 2018).

many barriers for reinsurance with too many rules. The reality was that if it became too complicated to do reinsurance in any territory, some of the high-quality securities would tend to withdraw their capacity.

## 8.8 INWARD REINSURANCE

### What were the rules in respect of inward acceptance of reinsurance?

As per the legal provisions of the reinsurance and coinsurance regulations, local insurers and reinsurers could accept inward reinsurance business from both local and foreign markets (ch. I, art. 5). While local reinsurers could retain all the inward reinsurance business or retrocede part of it, for local insurers they were required to retain all the inward reinsurance they might accept. The law did not specify if this referred to net retention of gross retention. It was not clear whether the policymakers were saying inward reinsurance business accepted by local insurers was supposed to be for ultimate net retention or if the local reinsurer could retain all the business but with the option of being able to protect their retention. It was not clear to us what were the reasons behind this specific restriction. Under normal circumstances, regulators were supposed to allow insurers to plan and place their required reinsurance structures depending on nature of business and their risk appetite.

## 8.9 RETROCESSION

It was also stated in the reinsurance and coinsurance regulations that local reinsurers could not retrocede back into the local market risks accepted from the local market (ch. I, art. 5, cl. 4). Furthermore, in the clause that followed, it was stated that local insurers were not to accept inward foreign reinsurance business of more than 10 per cent of their annual gross written premium income. This type of condition was potentially a useful measure aimed at ensuring prudence on the part of local insurers if they did decide to accept inward reinsurance from abroad. At the time of writing this book, we were not aware of any local insurer in Angola involved in the active underwriting of inward foreign reinsurance business.

# References

Africa Re (2015), *The African Insurance Regulatory Directory*, analysis prepared by Dr Schanz. Zurich: Alms and Company AG.

African Reinsurance Corporation (1976), *Establishment Agreement of the African Reinsurance Corporation of 24 February 1976.*

Bermuda Monetary Authority (2016), 'AAA Reinsurance Limited—2016 Financial Statements', http://www.bma.bm/Insurance/ CURRENT%20FULL%20FILINGS%20CLASS%203A/ AAA%20Reinsurance%20Limited%20-%202016%20Financial%20 Statements.pdf (accessed 8 May 2018).

Dias, Nélia Daniel (2012), *Legislação Financeira e dos Seguros.* Luanda: Texto Editores, Lda.

Hebo, Quingila (2018), 'Das 26 seguradoras licenciadas 19 podem fechar brevemente', *Expansão*, 9 February 2018.

Hossi, Emerson (2018). 'Fórum Segurador Oil & Gas Debate Repartição do Know-How Técnico no Sector Petrolífero', *Notícias de Angola*, https://www.noticiasdeangola.co.ao/forum-segurador-oilgas-debate-reparticao-do-know-how-tecnico-no-sector-petrolifero/ (accessed 15 June 2018).

Irukwu, J. O. (1998), *Insurance Management in Africa.* Lagos: BIMA Publications.

Macauhub (2018), 'Angola's National Reinsurance Company Starts Operating in 2018', https://macauhub.com.mo/2018/06/07/pt-empresa-nacional-de-resseguros-de-angola-comeca-a-funcionar-em-2018/ (accessed on 15 June 2018).

Mumenthaler, C. (2017), 'Open Markets: The Key to Enhancing Societal Resilience', *Reactions CEO Risk Forum.* London: Goran Pandzic. Summer 2017.

# Chapter 9

# INSURANCE CONTRACTS AND RATING GUIDELINES

Following our discussion on coinsurance and reinsurance, we shall now discuss the regulations regarding insurance contracts and tariff systems. In Angola, like most other territories worldwide, the policymakers found it necessary to pass specific regulations on insurance contracts, given their unique nature compared to contracts of all other types of business. As we noted in Chapter 3, the Portuguese Commercial Code of 1888 was the basis of the principles of insurance and legal elements of insurance. Besides the rules and regulations regarding insurance contracts, we shall discuss the regulations in respect of rating guidelines in Angola.

## 9.1 LEGAL CONDITIONS OF INSURANCE CONTRACTS

The insurance contract regulations[38] (*regulamento sobre o contrato de seguros*) were governed by decree (*decreto*) no. 2/02 of 11 February 2002 (Dias, 2012: 310–325). We shall not discuss all the clauses of this regulatory frame but rather focus on some of the key features of this piece of legislation. The Regulations on Conditions of Access and Conduct of Business of Insurers also had legal conditions relating to insurance contracts and collection of premiums. We shall make appropriate references for some of the key areas covered in both regulations in respect of insurance contracts.

---

[38] We shall use this brief name to refer to this piece of legislation.

## What were the rules regarding currency of an insurance contract?

According to the insurance contract regulations, insurance contracts could be denominated in the national currency (*moeda nacional*) of Angola or in foreign currency (*moeda estrangeira*), in accordance with the monetary and foreign exchange legislation of the country (ch. I, s. I, art. 1). However, for purposes of accounts and of calculation of statistical and actuarial calculations, the documents were to be presented in the national currency. It was prohibited to compel any policyholder to insure in a foreign currency by refusing to issue a policy in the national currency.

We should note that the question of currency was one of the major current problems due to a foreign-exchange crisis experienced in Angola from 2016. Insurers found themselves exposed to significant foreign-exchange losses for their net account. The major challenge was that, at the beginning of the policy period, insurers would quote in local currency and receive the appropriate premium. In cases where the risks in question would have been reinsured abroad, they needed to convert the sums insured and premium at the exchange rate at the time of placement of risk. However, due to a shortage of foreign currency, local insurers would find themselves only able to do the transfers to reinsurers many months afterwards. Unfortunately, at the time of doing the transfer, the commercial bank would want the insurer to provide a top-up of additional funds required as a result of depreciation of the local currency whilst waiting for clearance. The insurer could no longer go back to the insured to demand more premium and could also not pay reinsurers less than the agreed amount of premium.

## What were the rules regarding insurance contract wordings?

The insurance contract regulations contained specific provisions to be applied for insurance contracts and all other elements of an insurance agreement (ch. I, s. I, art. 4 & 8). It was stated in the regulations that an insurance contract was supposed to always be reduced to a written agreement. The wording of the insurance contract (*redacção do contrato de seguros*) and all other elements of an insurance contract were supposed to be in Portuguese and written in a legible, clear, and simple form. We believed that these were vital conditions for protection of consumers. We were aware that for certain types of specialist policies, it was difficult to get wordings in Portuguese, and that insurance contracts for major construction projects, oil and gas operations, mining, marine, and aviation were mainly written in English.

## What were the rules regarding standard obligatory policy wordings?

We noted that specified types of insurance were supposed to be underwritten subject to standard obligatory policy wordings (*apólice uniforme*), as stated in the Insurance Contract Regulations of 11 February 2002 (Ch. V, art. 52). We were aware that standard market policy wordings were used for obligatory types of insurance, such as WCA insurance and motor third-party liability. We also noted that failure to comply with the requirement to use approved standard obligatory market wordings was subject to fines and penalties, as defined in the sanctions regime, decree no. 7/02 of 9 April 2002 (ch. II, s. I, art. 3, cl. 2i.).

We would like to state that we were aware of the benefits of setting standard insurance contracts for both the sellers and buyers of insurance. Some insurance market observers argued that, when insurers in the same market worked with standard policy wordings such as the Multi-mark III, it improved efficiency and clarity on scope of cover (FA News: 2007). At the same time, intermediaries and consumers of insurance could easily compare prices of different underwriters, since they would be comparing apples with apples. We agreed with the analysis of insurance marketing by Manuel Leiria (2013:69) who asserted that comparing insurance product was a complex process that most consumers were not prepared to do on their own. He argued that most people wanted to focus only on the simplest aspect: the price.

Notwithstanding the support by some market observers of the practice of standardising insurance wordings, the insurance market of South Africa abandoned Multi-mark III in 2007 due to concerns that this was an 'anti-competitive' practice. Under the South African competition regulatory framework, it was not permitted for competing companies to have agreements or forms of coordination, even if the business operators actually believed that they would be able to attain efficiency for the benefit of consumers. Given that Angola had recently passed new competition regulations guided by similar principles, we were curious to see how the policymakers would handle some of the issues in the insurance legislative framework. The requirements on standard wordings, fixed rates, prescribed administration fees, and many other rules and regulations in the legal framework could be seen as part of anticompetitive behaviour.

## What were the legal requirements for proposal forms?

As defined in the insurance contract regulations, proposal forms were an essential part of the legal requirements for a valid insurance contract (ch. I, s. II, art. 9). The insured entity was required by law to complete an insurance proposal form in full, responding truthfully to all questions. It was stated that an insurance agreement was concluded upon receipt by the insured of a communication of acceptance of the proposal form. It was also stipulated that the proposer would be considered as accepted and covered if there was no communication from the insurer within fifteen days after submission of the completed form (ch. I, s. II, art. 10).

# 9.2 INSURANCE PREMIUM

## What were the rules regarding premium collection?

The insurance contract regulations provided legal provisions regarding premium collection (ch. I, s. III, art. 17). Full premium for the entire period of cover was due to the insurer at the time of signing of the insurance contract. In the case of payment by instalments, the first portion was payable at the beginning of the insurance contracts and the balance of payments as per the dates established in the insurance policy documents. Lack of payment of the agreed-upon premium or instalment by the agreed-upon due date would constitute default of payment by the insured, and the insurer would be entitled to suspend insurance cover (ch. I, s. III, art. 18). The insurer was supposed to advise the insured of suspension of cover (*suspensão de garantias do contrato*) by registered letter and grant another period for payment of amounts due. After expiration of the additional payment period, the insurer could cancel the policy (*rescindir o contrato*).

After cancellation of the policy, the insurer could charge a premium for time on risk before cancellation.

Furthermore, we should note that the Regulations on Conditions of Access and Conduct of Business of Insurers, as covered in decree no. 5/03 of 24 January 2003, provided further rules on accounting for uncollected premium. Insurers were required to setup receivable premium provisions (*provisão para prémios em cobrança*) following a model of calculation annexed to the regulations. Reports on this provision were to be submitted to the insurance regulators by 30 April of each year (ch. VI, art. 28).

### What was the standard collection period for premiums?

The Regulations on Conditions of Access and Conduct of Business of Insurers also provided legal conditions for premium collections. It was stated in these regulations that the standard time period for collection of premiums was supposed to be thirty days from the date of the conclusion of the insurance agreement (ch. VI, art. 24). It was also noted that the specific collection period was to be specified in the general policy wording (*condiçoes gerais*) as well as the specific insurance schedule (*condições particulares*). If the premium was not paid by the due date, the regulations provided a standard notice period of thirty days (ch. VI, art. 23). Therefore, it was our understanding that the maximum period within which there was supposed to be collection of premiums was a maximum of sixty days in total. The first thirty days were the standard collection time, and then there was supposed to be an additional thirty-days' notice period if there was no payment by the original due date.

## 9.3 CLAIMS

### What were the claim notification regulations?

The Regulations on Conditions of Access and Conduct of Business of Insurers provided clear timelines for claim notification (ch. I, s. III, art. 19). In the event of occurrence of a claim, the insured was required to notify the insurer within a period of eight days from the date of occurrence of the claim or from the date when the insurer become aware of it. This period of claim notification was in alignment with the one set in the Commercial Code of 1888 (vol. II heading XV, ch. II, s. I, art. 440). The insured was to provide all information required by the insurer on the claim and was supposed to complete truthfully and in full all claims documents presented by the insurer.

We believed that a claims notification period of eight days was very strict and would tend to give insurers more space to reject claims due to late notification, even if there was no prejudice to the insurer. The standard claim notification period in some of the principal insurance policy documents applied in southern Africa was usually thirty days. In other markets such as South Africa, there were policies that referred to a 'reasonable' claim notification period. The key concern was that even if the claim notification came one year after occurrence, there could be a valid explanation as to why the insured would have failed to notify the insurer immediately. We observed in a case of a late claim notification that the ombudsman for short-term insurance in South Africa informed an insurer that it could not reject a claim if there was no 'actual prejudice' suffered by the insurer (OSTI, 2016: 7).

# 9.4 INSURANCE RATING GUIDELINES

The rating systems of insurance business were subject to regulation as provided for in executive decree no. 58/02 of 5 December 2002 (de Abreu, 2014: 153–258). We shall refer to these regulations as insurance rating systems guidelines (*normas sobre sistemas de tarifas de seguros*). This piece of legislation was passed in the transition period when insurance-business activity was being transformed from a monopoly to an open insurance market. In this period, one of the principal preoccupations of policymakers was creating a business environment conducive to healthy competition and ensuring financial soundness of the emerging insurance market, as outlined in the preamble of this piece of law. We shall now discuss some of the key features of these regulations.

## Which types of insurance were subject to a fixed tariff system?

All obligatory types of insurance and specified classes of insurance business were supposed to be subject to fixed tariffs (*tarifas uniformes*), as defined in Article 1 of the regulations on Insurance Rating Systems Guidelines. The classes of insurance specified in Annex I of these regulations were WCA insurance, basic fire insurance, and marine hull and motor insurance. As discussed in Chapter 8, there were eleven types of obligatory insurance in Angola. We were not able to locate the applicable rates for them according to the rules of this regulatory framework.

Furthermore, we should note that the idea of fixing premium rates for obligatory types of insurance was not unique to Angola. A number of African insurance markets also had fixed insurance premium rates for obligatory types of insurance. In *Development of Insurance in Mozambique* (Muchena, 2018: 112), we observed that there existed a standard market agreement fixing prices for the motor third-party liability insurance for foreign registered vehicles entering Mozambique. As we discussed in the previous chapter, it appeared that insurance companies tended not to strictly adhere to the rating guidelines (AXCO, 2011: 6 and AXCO, 2018: 31).

## What were the rules regarding registration of all rating systems?

Insurance companies were required to submit for approval by the insurance regulator all their rating systems for all their insurance business besides the types of insurance subject to fixed rates. In order to avoid repeated alterations of approved rating tables, insurers could indicate in their rating systems minimum and maximum range within which they could deviate from their defined rates (art. 7). We considered this to be one of the highest levels of control by regulatory authorities of pricing of insurance in the SADC region. We also believed that with modernisation of the insurance business, there would be adoption of a more dynamic rating system that would require a more refined regulatory approach. This was one of the issues that would be resolved if the approach to insurance supervision were to be changed from the traditional compliance-based model to risk-based one in the planned reform of the insurance legal framework. With risk-based supervision, the emphasis is not on requiring submission of specific rates charged by insurers. The requirement would be for underwriters to present their rating models and explanation of the principles driving the pricing mechanism.

Israel Muchena

## What were the fixed rates of administration fees defined in the regulations?

We also noted that the regulations of the insurance rating guidelines also defined the fixed amount of administration fees (*encargos*) to be charged by insurers for each type of insurance business. We would like to note that we also saw the practice of charging of administration fees in Mozambique (Muchena: 2018: 91). In the legal framework of Mozambique, this fee was viewed as part of the income of the insurer. There was no specific legal requirement which specified that it was supposed to be charged. The key difference was that in the case of Angola, the minimum rates were defined in the insurance legislation (art. 11, cl. 1). However, we were aware that not all insurers were applying in all cases these fixed rates of administration fees. The rates defined in the regulations were as follows:

- life (*vida*), 1.5 per cent
- Workmen's Compensation Act insurance (*acidente de trabalho*), 20 per cent
- personal accident (*acidentes pessoais*), 20 per cent
- travel insurance (*acidentes pessoais em viagens*), 20 per cent
- health (*saúde*), 15 per cent
- motor (*automóvel*), 20 per cent
- marine hull (*marítimo cascos*), 20 per cent
- marine cargo (*marítimo cargas*), 20 per cent
- professional indemnity (*responsbilidade civil profissional*), 15 per cent
- aviation cargo (aéreo cargas), 20 per cent
- aviation hull (aéreo cascos), 15 per cent
- aviation liability (*aéreo responsailidade civil*), 15 per cent
- aviation crew (*aéreo tripulações*), 15 per cent
- fire (*incêndio*), 20 per cent
- glass (*vidros*), 20 per cent
- theft (*roubo*), 20 per cent
- natural perils (*cataclismos naturais*), 20 per cent
- construction and erection (*construções e montagens*), 20 per cent
- oil and gas (*petrolífero*), 10 per cent
- general liability (*responsbilidade civil geral*), 20 per cent

# 9.5 RECOMMENDED NATIONAL MORTALITY TABLES

## Where were the recommended Angolan mortality tables located?

As we noted in Chapter 2, the construction of the first mortality tables in Europe in the Early Modern Epoch was one of the key milestones in the history of development of insurance. The regulatory legislation on Insurance Rating Systems Guidelines (ch. IV) contained recommended mortality tables (*tábuas de mortalidade*) to be applied in Angola (de Abreu, 2014: 1188–1189). The use of any form of mortality table required authorisation by the insurance regulator (app. I, ch. I, art. 4, cl. 1). We believed that it was important that there was a possibility for an insurer to apply other models of mortality tables, if approved by the regulator.

# 9.6 REJECTED OBLIGATORY INSURANCE RISKS

We shall now discuss a circular from the insurance regulator which also impacted on insurance contracts, as per circular no. 01/ISS/MF/10 of 2 March 2010. It was a directive giving the insurance regulator authority to nominate an insurer and indicate terms and conditions to be applied on contracts in respect of motor third-party liability insurance rejected by all insurance companies in the market. According to Article 4 of this circular, the principal objective of the regulator for all risks rejected by all the market was to spread the risk amongst all the insurers underwriting the motor insurance business.

We were not aware if there had been cases where the regulator had instructed the insurance market to cover any risk that had been rejected by all insurers in the market. As indicated in the preamble of this directive, the regulatory authorities were aware that part of the reasons why insurers could decline to insure a given person was due to poor claims experience or, in some cases, poor upkeep of the vehicle that was subject to insurance. If the market believed a certain risk was uninsurable and the state still wanted it to be covered, then, the state was to consider setting up a fund for these types of cases. However, we believed that, instead of forcing the private insurance market to try to cover a person or vehicle that did not meet conditions to be insurable, the most appropriate solution was to prevent that person from driving. In our view, even the transfer to a public fund of such exposure would probably not be the best solution for spending scarce resources.

# References

AXCO (2011), *Angola: Non-Life Insurance Market Report*. London: AXCO Insurance Information Services.

AXCO (2018), *Angola: Non-Life Insurance Market Report*. London: AXCO Insurance Information Services.

de Abreu, Ana Edith Viegas (2014), *100 Anos de Legislação de Seguros em Angola*. Luanda: Edições Chá de Caxinde.

Dias, Nélia Daniel (2012), *Legislação Financeira e dos Seguros*. Luanda: Texto Editores, Lda.

FA News (2007), 'No winners as Multimark III disappears', https://www. fanews.co.za/article/magazine-archives-fanews-fanuus/60/short-term/1317/no-winners-as-multimark-iii-disappears/10008 (accessed on 5 June 2018).

Leiria, Manuel (2013), *Marketing de Seguros*. Lisboa: Escola Editora.

Muchena, Israel (2018), *Development of Insurance in Mozambique*. Bloomington: AuthorHouse.

OSTI (2016), *The Ombudsman's Briefcase Newsletter*, March 2016, issue no. 1, Johannesburg: The Ombudsman for Short-Term Insurance, https://www.masthead.co.za/wp-content/uploads/2016/04/OSTI-Briefcase-Newsletter-1-2016-1.pdf (accessed on 15 June 2018).

Chapter 10

# THE EMERGING INSURANCE MARKET

We shall now discuss the key characteristics of the structure of the emerging insurance market in Angola following the transition from a monopoly to a market based on competition. We shall look at some of the new associations that have been established to date and evaluate the performance of this market as per the published reports of the insurance regulator. We shall also review other key services and institutions that were required for effective operation of the insurance market.

## 10.1 STRUCTURE OF THE ANGOLAN INSURANCE MARKET

As we have noted in this book, the insurance legal framework was based on legislation from the national lawmakers, including ARSEG, the insurance regulator, which also had authority to issue regulatory legislation consisting of circulars, notices, directives, and guidelines. The insurance regulator was responsible for oversight of the different insurance activities. As illustrated in Figure 8, insurance business from the different market segments was placed directly or through intermediaries. Insurance companies retained some of the risks and reinsured the balance directly or through reinsurance brokers. We noted that at this stage, the reinsurers for Angola were located in regional and international markets.

## Figure 8: Structure of the Angolan Insurance Market

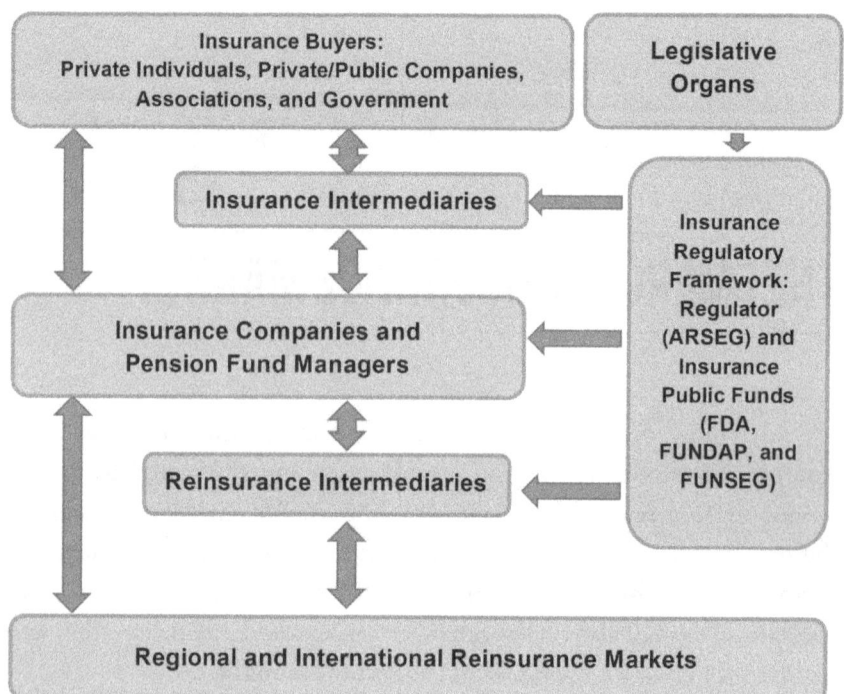

## How many insurance companies were registered in Angola?

As outlined in Appendix I, there were twenty-seven registered insurance companies at the end of 2018. As we discussed in Chapter 5, a handful of these registered companies appeared to be dormant licenses. Furthermore, over the past four years, there were an additional six pending applications that appeared to have executed part of the registration process, as follows:

- Seventrust Companhia de Seguros, SA, as per ministerial decree no. 1452/14 of 8 July 2014 and correction rectification order no. 11/14 of 8 July 2014.
- Prefira Seguros, SA, as per ministerial decree no. 1451/14 of 8 July, 2014
- Intercontiseguros Companhia de Seguros, SA, as per ministerial decree no. 318/15 of 19 October 2015
- Zurich Angola Seguros, SA, as per ministerial decree no. 113/16 of 24 March 2016

- Mais Seguros, SA, as per ministerial decree no. 253/17 of 30 May 2017
- Nito Kafundala Seguros, SA, as per ministerial decree no. 364/17 of 28 July 2017

We learned from our discussions with some of the operators in this market that there was a major concern that it was becoming saturated with too many insurers and intermediaries with limited knowledge of the insurance business. Most of the existing insurers were not even executing basic business functions, such as issuing of audited financial accounts (Hebo, 2018). This problem was echoed by Michael Duncan, managing director of Marsh Africa Region, who observed that in Africa, in general, too many licensed entities 'often lack[ed] the necessary security and expertise' (AIO, 2017: 45). He argued that for better performance of the insurance markets, it was essential to have 'fewer and stronger players'.

It was on this basis that it was widely anticipated that there would be some consolidations in the future. We believed that such a trend was also likely to affect Angola. We had already noted the impact of this emerging trend following reports of the acquisition of Saham by the South Africa insurer Sanlan for a value of US$1 billion (Dludla and Abdennebi, 2018). The Angolan subsidiary of Saham was one of the large insurers in the network of this group, which was represented in twenty-six countries.

## What was the make-up of the registered insurance companies?

From the twenty-seven registered insurers as noted above, twenty-three of them were local Angolan brands. Given the strong economic base of Angola, most of the capital in the insurance market was from local investors. As we discussed in Chapter 1, the first two insurers were public companies. Besides the involvement of the state, the most dominant source of local investments in insurance business were major local banking groups.

As far as foreign direct investment was concerned, only three insurers had a majority shareholding of foreign insurance groups. From these three insurers with a significant foreign direct investment, two companies were part of Portuguese financial groups. Saham Angola was the only insurer in Angola that was part of a group with a presence in any other African country. As we discussed above, a major South African financial group acquired Saham insurance operations, including the license in Angola, in 2018. We believed that the make-up of the Angolan insurance market would continue to change and that there would be other major acquisitions. We believed that these were part of the critical ingredients for the development of this market.

### How many insurance intermediaries were registered in Angola?

The insurance and reinsurance intermediation segment consisted of the following licensed entities listed on the website of the Angola insurance regulator as of 30 June 2018:
- 399 individual insurance agents
- 56 intermediaries registered as legal entities (*pessoas colectivas*), as per Appendix VI (please note that some of the intermediaries had licenses to do both insurance and reinsurance intermediation)
- No intermediaries focussed on only reinsurance brokerage

## 10.2 PROFESSIONAL ASSOCIATIONS AND TRAINING INSTITUTIONS

### Was there an insurance association in Angola?

There existed an Association of Insurance Companies of Angola, referred to in Portuguese as Associação de Seguradoras de Angola (ASAN). It was formed in 2010. As defined in the statutes[39] of ASAN, the main goals of the association were to protect and promote the interests of the insurance market. We should also note that as per the organization's code of conduct,[40] one of the purposes of the association was to promote strict compliance with rules of protection of competition and all the legislation of Angola. We believed that an effective insurance association could play a useful role in key activities such as skills development and market reports

---

[39] As presented on the ASAN website, http://www.asan.co.ao/index.php?page=estatutos (accessed 20 February 2018).
[40] . As posted on the ASAN website, http://www.asan.co.ao/index.php?page=conduta, (accessed 20 February 2018).

as well as the setting up of market agreements in appropriate areas without engaging in anticompetitive actions. One of the agreements where insurers could collaborate without appearing to undermine interests of consumers was in setting up of knock-for-knock agreements (Irukwu, 2007: 25)

## Did an Association of Insurance Brokers exist in Angola?

We observed that circular no. 06/ISS.MF/10 of 2 August 2010 on insurance intermediation stated that the insurance regulator could sign cooperation agreements with the Association of Insurance Intermediaries (ch. VI, art. 16), referred to in the circular as Associação de Mediadores de Seguros de Angola (AMSA). However, it did not appear that the statutes of this entity had been formally approved, and it appeared that it was still to be formally established. In our view, it would be a beneficial development if a body representing intermediaries could be formally established.

## Was there an insurance training institution in Angola?

We observed that Angola did not have an accredited professional insurance training institution. However, we were aware that since 2015, there existed a company offering, amongst other services, training for the insurance market. The statutes of this entity known as Academia de Seguros e Fundos de Pensões (ASFP) were published in the *Government Gazette* on 18 June 2015. The academy was set up in the form of a private limited company (art. 1) owned by two identified founding shareholders (art. 3).

We should note that most of the training institutes in Africa and most international insurance markets tend to be non-profit organisations, and the founding members were usually the operators in the insurance sector. Nevertheless, it appeared that the academy had been fairly active in executing training initiatives with the support of specialist professional personnel from ENSA and the auditing firm PwC for the first series of courses (Sousa, 2016). We also noted that this entity had already arranged workshops for the insurance sector and had played an active role in insurance awareness campaigns.

## Were there enough actuaries in Angola?

According to Nuno Matos, the consulting actuary at PwC Angola, there was a critical shortage of actuarial skills in Angola (Hebo, 2018: 19). He indicated that he was aware of only three or four actuaries in Angola. That was not enough, given the growing number of licensed insurance companies. Furthermore, when the authorities referred to plans to adopt modern insurance regulatory frameworks, there would be even more demand for such skills. We believed that it was critical for key stakeholders to consider this situation could be addressed.

# 10.3 INSURANCE CONSUMER WATCHDOG

## Was there an insurance consumer watchdog in Angola?

We were aware that there were high levels of customer dissatisfaction with a number of the licensed insurers, pension-fund management companies, and public insurance mechanisms. As we saw in Chapter 4, it appeared that nobody could trace any claim that the Motor Guarantee Fund had ever paid. The insurance regulator also made reference to many complaints against several of the companies in the preamble to notice (*aviso*) no. 1/15 of 13 October 2015. This notice was intended to establish rules and procedures to be followed in the handling of complaints lodged by policyholders, insured parties, beneficiaries, and injured third parties. In the same preamble, it was asserted that consumer protection (*defesa do consumidor*) was the 'primordial objective' of the regulatory body. This objective was viewed by policymakers as a central part of the function of supervision of market conduct.

As we discussed in Chapter 4, contrary to emerging global approaches, in Angola the insurance regulator was still responsible for both prudential and market-conduct supervision. We would like to highlight that we could already see some potential conflicting interests on the part of the insurance regulator. The Motor Guarantee Fund, which was the subject of many complaints, was supposed to have been set up and run by the regulator. How could consumers be assured of a fair hearing of their grievances against this fund? Notwithstanding this issue, we believed that there were useful rules and procedures in the directive regarding the handling of complaints, as we discussed in Chapter 5.

## What were the rules and regulations regarding third-party administrators and assistance companies providing service to the insurance market?

We could not trace any specific rules and regulations in the insurance legal framework involving third party administrators and assistance companies providing service to the local insurance market. We were able to trace a handful of TPAs already involved in marketing and administration of health insurance, which was one of the fastest growing classes of insurance in Angola. We believed that this could be one of the areas that could be reviewed in the planned reforms of the insurance regulatory framework.

## 10.4 PERFORMANCE OF THE INSURANCE MARKET

The most recent market report on the Angolan insurance market was published in 2015. The report was compiled by the insurance regulator in collaboration with PwC Angola. The report provided comprehensive information on the performance of the top ten Angolan insurance companies in the period 2011 to 2013. However, the key challenge was that there had been a significant change in the insurance market in the period between 2013 and now. This tended to limit the benefit to be derived from this report. We hoped that more up-to-date reports would be available in the future.

According to the 2015 market report of ARSEG, only eleven of the seventeen licensed operators submitted appropriate financial information as required by law. From these companies that submitted the required information on their accounts, the total premium income of the top ten insurers in Angola in 2013 for life and non-life was Angolan Kwanza 97.6 billion. This was the equivalent of US$997.45 million as per the exchange rate at the end of 2013. The market shares of the top five largest insurers in 2013 were as shown in Figure 9.

**Figure 9: Market Share of Top Five Angolan Insurers in 2013**

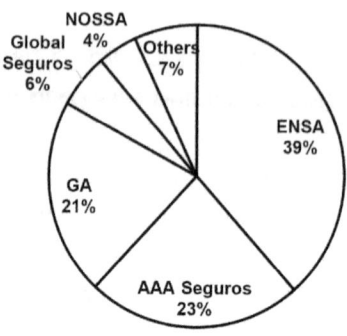

Following the nomination of ENSA as the leader for oil and gas business in Angola in March 2016, we expected that this state-owned insurer would have remained the largest insurer in Angola up to the period of the publishing of this case study in 2018. We shall continue to monitor developments in this exciting emerging frontier market. We also noted that with the recent formation of an insurance association, the market would be more organized and would be able to contribute to efforts aimed at improving the rate of penetration of insurance.

# 10.5 FINANCIAL SOUNDNESS OF THE MARKET

At the time of writing this book, some market observers were concerned about the risk of financial soundness of some of the operators in Angolan insurance. According to the interview published in the newspaper *Expansão*, the actuarial consultant from PwC could affirm the financial soundness of only seven of the registered insurance companies in Angola (Hebo, 2018: 18). These were the only companies that were appropriately preparing their annual finance accounts with appropriate reserves as required in the insurance legislative framework and having the same accounts audited without qualifications and published in full compliance with the current legislation of Angola.

Following the above observations, the insurance regulator made some communications confirming confidence in the financial soundness of the local insurance market (AngoNotícias, 2018). The authorities were of the view that they were carrying out the required supervision to monitor the risk of insolvency. They admitted that they were aware that some of the companies were going through financial difficulties due to the current economic and financial crisis. There were no comments regarding the fact that many of the insurance companies were not publishing appropriately audited financial accounts as required by law.

# 10.6 MARKET SATURATION

In addition to the discussions of financial soundness presented above, we would like to look at the issue of market saturation. As noted in *The African Insurance Regulatory Directory* (2015: 17), some of the regulators in Africa were of the opinion that 'consolidation' of insurers could be one of the solutions to address the problem of low average premium income per company. The issue of adequate volumes of premium was a critical measure for financial viability of an insurer and was linked to the financial capacity to generate funds in order to raise adequate levels of reserves to cover future liabilities. Some of the market observers in Angola were concerned about the high number of licenses when most of the operators appeared not to be financial sound operations (Hebo, 2018).

We observed that one of the key pillars of the current development policy of the lawmakers for the insurance market was the concept of obligatory coinsurance for key types of businesses, including aviation, oil, and gas. We noted that there was no clarity on how the current model was supposed to work. Following the transition of leadership from AAA Seguros to ENSA Seguros, it was hoped by the policymakers that an appropriate model would be developed. At the time of writing this book, it did not appear that there was clarity on what was going to be the new market model. As we discussed in Chapter 8, some of the key stakeholders were expressing dissatisfaction with the current policy of having one leader handling all the work in underwriting and reinsurance of all the risks in this sector. They felt that in such a model, there was no transfer of skills to the rest of the market.

## 10.7 PERFORMANCE OF INTERMEDIARIES

From our review of the insurance market reports of Angola as well as the website and publications of the insurance regulator, we were not able to locate reports on performance of insurance intermediaries in Angola. We also observed that it was not only Angola that did not have this type of analysis. Most insurance markets in Africa faced a similar challenge of having reports focussing only on insurance companies. We would like to recommend that the Angolan market could consider including sections in their market reports on performance of insurance intermediaries, like the case of the report from the Portuguese insurance regulator (ASF, 2007).

## 10.8 FINANCIAL INCLUSION

We would like to also note that in Angola, as in all other developing world economies, there was a growing interest in the concept of 'financial inclusion' and microinsurance, or insurance for the majority low-income population. Due to this emerging global preoccupation in respect of inclusive growth, we believed that it was crucial for policymakers in Angola to look at both the growth of insurance and the nature of development in this activity. We had observed that up to the end of 2016, the growth of the insurance sector of this country to an annual turnover of more than US$1 billion had been mainly due to a high volume of premium generated by oil and gas risks. There existed significant potential for expansion of insurance services into largely untapped areas, such as the informal sector, small-to-middle sized enterprises, agriculture, personal lines, life, and health.

# References

Africa Re (2015), *The African Insurance Regulation Directory*, analysis prepared by Dr Schanz, Zurich: Alms and Company AG.

African Insurance Organisation (2017), *Africa Insurance Barometer 2017*, prepared by Dr Schanz. Zurich: Alms and Company AG.

AngoNotícias (2018b), 'Seguros: Regulador diz que não há risco de falência', 14/04/2018, http://www.angonoticias.com/Artigos/item/57664/seguros-regulador-diz-que-nao-ha-risco-de-falencia

ASF (2007), '*Relatório do Setor Segurador e dos Fundos de Pensões*', http://www.asf.com.pt/NR/exeres/9761BAC3-D3A7-4DEB-928C-C1FAAB73D544.htm (accessed 26 April 2018).

Dludla, Nqobile, and Zakia Abdennebi (2018), 'Sanlam Buys out Morocco's SAHAM Finances in $1 Billion Africa Expansion', *Reuters*, https://www.reuters.com/article/us-sanlam-semil-stake/sanlam-buys-out-moroccos-saham-finances-in-1-billion-african-expansion-idUSKCN1GK0LJ (accessed 15 June 2018).

Hebo, Quingila (2018), '*Das 26 seguradoras licenciadas 19 podem fechar brevemente*', *Expansão*, 9 February 2018.

Irukwu, J. O. (2007), *Fundamentals of Insurance Law*. London: Witherbys Printing Ltd.

Sousa, Rosimaria (2018), 'Primeira Academia de Seguros Abre Portas', *Mercado*, http://www.mercado.co.ao/capital-humano/upgrade/jack-ma-timoneiro-do-e-commerce/ (accessed 20 May 2018).

# Chapter 11

# GENERAL LEGAL FRAMEWORK FOR DOING BUSINESS

Following our review of the legislation relating to the insurance business and related activities, we should now review in this chapter the other key pieces of law that affected all business activities in general. We should note that the rules and regulations reviewed were in alignment with the principal guidelines of the National Policy for Private Investment (*Linhas Mestras da Política Nacional de Investimento Privado*), as per presidential decree no. 181/15 of 30 September 2015. The guidelines in this policy document were aligned to the emerging national economic policy as the country shifted to a market-led economy. The main objectives of this policy framework were as follows:

- to attract private domestic investment and foreign direct investment, given that Angola had opted for a national development policy of market economy
- to develop local economic production in order to support a strategy of gradual import substitution
- to promote exports of products with a higher local value-added
- to diversify the national economy in order to reduce excessive dependence on oil and gas

We shall now discuss the key pieces of legislation that were passed to support this national policy framework for a market based on competition and private investments.

# 11.1 PRIVATE INVESTMENTS LAW

As part of the transition process to a market economy at the beginning of the twenty-first century, the Angolan National Parliament enacted a private investments legislation through law no. 11/03 of 13 March of 2003. This was followed by reforms in 2011 (law no. 20/11 of 20 May) and in 2015 (law no. 14/15 of 11 August). Then, as we were finalising the publishing of this book, there were further changes to private investment legislation, as provided for in law no. 10/18 of 26 June 2018. As noted in the preamble to the private investment law, the main goal of the policymakers was to create an environment that was conducive to business in order to promote and attract more private sector investments. Furthermore, we noted in the preamble to the 2018 investment law that the government was seeing its role as only that of an agent for promoting and regulation of socio-economic development.

## For which business activities was it obligatory to have a local partner?

This was one of the aspects where the 2018 private investment legislation was significantly different to that of 2015. The investment law of 2015 identified critical sectors where foreign investors were required to have an Angolan partner with at least 35 per cent of the capital and effective management participation (ch. III, art. 9). This condition was removed in the 2018 legislation. The only key protections maintained involved employment of local labour as well as training and development of local skills (ch. VII, art. 46, cl. 1). The same law permitted employment of qualified foreign workers subject to rigorous compliance with training and capacity building plans for Angolan workers as well as preparation for succession planning of local personnel (ch. VII, art. 46, cl. 2).

## Which private business investments qualified for investment incentives?

One of the most critical changes in the private investment legislation of 2018 was the removal of minimum amounts of investment required to qualify for incentives and benefits (ch. I, art. 2, cl. 1). In the private investment legislation of 2015, there was a requirement to invest a minimum of US$1 million for foreign investments and US$500,000 for domestic investments. We shall not review the details of the different types of incentives and benefits that were available for private investments. The key factors influencing levels of benefits in the new investment laws were whether the investment was in a priority sector and the zone in Angola where the investment was located (ch. V, art. 27). Priority sectors included education, agriculture, health, textiles, hospitality, construction, telecommunications, information technology, infrastructure, electricity, and waste removals (ch. V, art. 28).

## What rights did a foreign investor have in relation to profits and dividends?

According to the new private investments law, foreign investors had a right to make remittances abroad of dividends, profits distributed from the local company, royalties, and other investment returns (ch. V, s. I, art. 22). We were aware that foreign remittances were one of the major challenges for both business entities and private individuals. However, we noted that with the revision of the foreign exchange policy, the situation had started to improve in the beginning of the second half of 2018.

## What was the government agency responsible for private investments?

In the period of liberalization of the Angolan economy and opening up of the market to private sector competition, there were three key changes in the structure of the entities responsible for handling private investments, as summarized in Table 9. AIPEX, the Agency for Private Investment and Promotion of Exports, was the most recent agency created as we were completing the writing of this book. The government was aiming to reduce the bureaucracy involved in the process of registering new private investments.

**Table 9: Private Investment Agencies from 2003 to 2018**

| Year | Type of Private Investment Agency |
|------|-----------------------------------|
| 2003 | ANIP[1]—National Private Investment Agency (*Agência Nacional do Investimento Privado*) |

| 2015 | APIEX[2]—Agency for the Promotion of Investment and Exports (*Agência para a Promoção do Investimento e Exportações*) supported by the following units:<br>• UTAIs—provincial government technical units (*unidade técnica de apoio ao investidor*)<br>• UTAIPs—technical unit to support private investment (*unidade técnica de apoio ao investimento privado*) for projects of less than US$10 million<br>• UTIP—technical unit for private investments (*unidade técnica para o investimento privado*) for projects of US$10 million or more |
|------|------|
| 2018 | AIPEX[3]—Agency for Private Investment and Promotion of Exports (*Agência de Investimento Privado e Promoção das Exportações*) |

# 11.2 THE COMPETITION REGULATORY FRAMEWORK

Did Angola have a competition regulatory framework to protect and support competition of private business in the market?

Following the three phases of transformation of the Angolan political economy as described in Chapter 2, the regulatory framework to support the emerging policy from the early 1990s of a competition-based market was still a work in progress at the time of writing this book. The Competition Law (*Lei da Concorrência*) of Angola in the new dispensation was enacted through law no. 5/18 of 10 May 2018.[44] This legislation made provision for the establishment of a Competition Regulatory Authority (*Autoridade*

---

[41] Established in accordance with the private investments law no. 11/03 of 13 May 2003.

[42] Created in accordance with presidential decree no. 184/15 of 30 September 2015.

[43] Constituted as per presidential decree no. 81/18 of 19 March 2018, as consulted on the following website on 9 April 2018: https://www.lexlink.eu/FileGet. aspx?FileId=3006809.

[44] As downloaded from Lexlink, https://www.lexlink.eu/FileGet.aspx?FileId=3007948 (accessed 17 May 2018).

*Reguladora da Concorrência*) (ch. I, s. II, art. 4). It was supposed to be an autonomous regulatory body responsible for ensuring compliance with rules regarding competition.

Furthermore, in alignment with global-competition legal frameworks, the new competition legislation of Angola appropriately defined prohibited competition-restrictive practices (*prácticas restrictivas da concorrência*). If the regulatory framework was to be actually enforced, the insurance market would need to review some of the existing practices, such as the fixing of minimum premium rates for certain types of insurance, including even some classes of insurance that were not obligatory, as we discussed in Chapter 9. As we witnessed in Kenya, the Office of the Ombudsman challenged in court the practice of the local insurance regulator of issuing motor insurance underwriting guidelines aimed at fixing minimum amounts of premium (Wasuma, 2017a). In this specific case, the High Court of Kenya ruled that the insurance regulator did not have authority to fix insurance premiums (Wasuma, 2017b).

In addition, the new competition law contained compliance requirements for mergers and acquisitions, which could adversely affect competition in the insurance market. In order to complete the setting up of this regulatory framework, supporting regulations were needed to define, amongst other things, the criteria for determining forms of mergers and acquisitions that required prior clearance as defined in the new competition law (ch. III, art. 17). As far as governance and accountability was concerned, we hoped that this new body would follow the good examples of other more organised bodies, such as the Angolan stock exchange regulator, BODIVA, as per our discussions in Chapter 1.

## 11.3 COMMERCIAL COMPANIES LAW

The commercial companies law (*lei das sociedades comerciais*) no. 1/04 of 13 February 2004 was the main piece of legislation governing how business entities could be set up and how they were supposed to conduct business. It was a crucial piece of legislation for all entities or persons intending to do business in Angola. From the different types of companies that could be set up for business as defined in this law (heading

I, ch. I, art. 2), we noted that all insurance companies were registered as public limited companies,[45] as could be observed on the list of registered insurance companies in Appendix I.

# 11.4 TAX LAW

We shall now look at the tax system of Angola as presented in the national guideline from the national tax authority, Administração Geral Tributária (2017). According to the tax guideline from Deloitte (2017: 22), there were no tax treaties in place between Angola and other countries. In addition, Angola did not have Value Added Tax (VAT) up to the first half of 2018. We were aware that the Angolan lawmakers were considering plans to implement VAT for 2019 (Macauhub, 2018). Instead of VAT, Angola had been using a system of consumption tax that was applied on supply and importation of specified goods and services. The tax year in Angola was the calendar year.

### What were the key types of taxes applicable to persons and business entities?

It was not our intention in this book to provide all the details on the tax system of Angola. The key types of taxes for a natural person or individual (*pessoa singular*) and for legal entities (*pessoas colectivas*) were as summarized below:

- **Corporate tax** (*imposto industrial*) as provided for in law no. 19/14 of 22 October 2014:
  - o general tax rate: 30 per cent.
  - o reduced rate for the agricultural sector: 15 per cent
  - o special tax regimes applicable for petroleum and mining sector
  - o tax on occasional services for non-resident entities: 6.5 per cent[46]

---

[45] Referred to in Portuguese as *Sociedades Anónimas* (*SA*)

[46] It was important to note this tax for insurance operations given that in some cases, occasional service providers such as loss assessors and risk surveyors were contracted from abroad to assist in cases where there were no local skills to execute the required task.

- **Withholding tax** as also provided for in the above law:
  - o  dividends/profit-sharing rate: 10 per cent
  - o  payments for services rate: 6.5 per cent
- **Personal income tax code** (*código do imposto sobre os rendimentos do trabalho*) as provided for in law no. 18/14 of 22 October 2014:
  - o  tax rates from 7 per cent to a maximum of 17 per cent
  - o  minimum monthly tax free income: AOA 34,450
- **Stamp tax** (*imposto do selo*) as provided for in the presidential legislative decree (*decreto legislativo presidencial*) no. 3/14 of 21 October 2014:
  - o  applicable on insurance and other documents and financial instruments as defined in the law
  - o  rates varied from 0.1 per cent to 1 per cent
- **Social security:**[47]
  - o  employer contribution: 8 per cent
  - o  employee contribution: 3 per cent
- **Consumption tax** (*imposto de consumo*) as per presidential legislative decree (*decreto legislativo presidencial*) no. 3-A/14 of 21 October 2014 and presidential legislative decree no. 5/15 of 21 September 2014:
  - o  standard rate: 10 per cent
- **Customs and excise duties** (*direitos e outras imposições aduaneiras*) as stipulated in executive order (*decreto executivo*) no. 5/06 of 4 October 2006 and presidential legislative decree (*decreto legislativo presidencial*) no. 10/ 13 of 22 November 2013:
  - o  applicable on all imported goods
  - o  variable rates depending on classification of goods
- **Urban property tax** (*imposto predial urbano*) as per legislative decree (*diploma legislativo*) no. 4044 *nº.4044*) and law no. 18/11 of 21 April 2011 (*lei nº. 18/11 de 21 de Abril*):
  - o  rate: 25 per cent
  - o  applied on rental income less deductible expenses capped at 40 per cent of rental value

---

[47] We looked at some of the basic features of the social security system of Angola in Chapter 8, as part of obligatory forms of public insurance.

- **Property transfer tax** (*imposto de SISA*), as specified in legislative decree (*diploma legislativo)* no. 230 of 18 May 1931 and law no. 16/11 of 21 April 2011:
  - o  tax rate due from buyer: 2 per cent
  - o  acquisition of 50 per cent or more of a limited liability company owning immovable property carried liability of property transfer tax
- **Inheritance/estate tax** (*imposto sobre sucessões e doações*) as provided for in legislative decree (*diploma legislativo*) no. 230 of 18 May 1931 and law no. 16/11 of 21 April 2011 (*lei nº. 16/11, de 21 de Abril*):
  - o  variable rates and exemptions depending on relationship and values involved

In addition to the taxes noted above, there were also special sector-specific tax regimes, as follows:
- special contributions for banking operations
- special tax regime for the oil and gas sector and for mining

# 11.5 LABOUR LAW

The Labour Law (*Lei Geral do Trabalho*) of Angola, no. 2/2000 of 11 February 2000, had specific provisions relating to obligatory insurance. According to the labour law, all employers were required to insure all workers, apprentices, and trainees against work-related accidents and occupational illnesses (ch. V, s. I, art. 85, cl. 1). The type of insurance that was required in this case was referred to as the Workmen's Compensation Act (WCA) insurance.[48] We discussed this type of insurance and other forms of obligatory insurance of this market in Chapter 7.

---

[48]  Referred to in Portuguese as Seguro de Acidentes do Trabalho e Doenças Profissionais.

# 11.6 FOREIGN EXCHANGE LAW

Following our reference to foreign exchange under the economic review in Chapter 1, we shall now briefly discuss key conditions of this law affecting insurance and reinsurance. The foreign exchange law (*lei cambial*) no. 5/97 of 27 June 1997 provided rules and regulations for handling foreign exchange in Angola. We would like to note that this was an essential piece of legislation given that one of the most critical conditions for effective insurance markets was the ability for insurers to place reinsurance in international markets and carry out respective premium remittances.

In view of the fact that there was no adequate local financial capacity and as part of effective management of risk by underwriters to avoid financial ruin, access to foreign reinsurance markets was indispensable. The Angolan insurance market required a significant amount of reinsurance, especially given the dominance of the oil and gas sector. Compared to the minimum capital of an insurance company of $10 million, some of the principal oil and gas risks in Angola had values at risk of as much as US$5 billion.

## What transactions were subject to the foreign exchange law?

According to the foreign exchange law, all commercial and financial transactions that could affect or have potential to affect the balance of payments of the country were subject to the foreign exchange law (ch. I, art. 1). When insurance companies in Angola needed to make payments of reinsurance premiums abroad or make recoveries from reinsurance markets on claims in Angola, such operations were part of what were defined as foreign exchange transactions as defined in this law (ch. II, art 5).

## Which entity was responsible for clearance of foreign exchange transactions?

According to the foreign exchange law, Banco Nacional de Angola (BNA), the central bank of Angola, was the entity responsible for clearance of all foreign exchange transactions (ch. I, art. 3). As noted in the same article, BNA also had authority to delegate part of its functions to appropriate entities. We should note that as part of a process of reducing the bureaucracy involved in applying for clearance of foreign transfers, the Central Bank announced in 2018 a set of new rules allowing commercial banks to handle part of the clearance process.

## 11.7 CIVIL LAW

For purposes of civil law (*código civil*), Angola was still relying on the Portuguese civil law (*código civil Português*) that was enacted in 1966 and subsequent amendments. The civil law provided the legal basis for critical conditions such as legal liability (vol. II, heading I, ch. II, s. V, sub-sec. I, art. 483), prescription of the right to indemnity (vol. II, heading I, ch. II, s. V, sub-s. I, art. 498), liability for damages caused by vehicles (vol. II, heading I, ch. II, s. V, sub-s. II, art. 503). We also noted that civil Law stated that fire insurance was obligatory for buildings (vol. III, heading II, ch. VI, s. III, art. 1429).

## 11.8 EASE OF DOING BUSINESS

Following our review of key pieces of law for doing business in Angola, we would like to conclude this chapter with a discussion of the general issue of ease of doing business in Angola. We would like to note that in the 2017 Ease of Doing Business Ranking of the World Bank, Angola came in at 182 out of the 190 economies surveyed (World Bank, 2017: 7). Angola also had very low scores in the 'economic freedom' score of the Heritage Foundation (2018: 78–79). For 2018, it was ranked 40 out of the 47 countries in the sub-Saharan region. The economic freedom status of Angola was defined as 'repressed'.

It was noted in the Heritage Foundation survey that the government had initiated 'modest reforms' in an effort to bring about required changes. However, 'pervasive corruption' and 'institutional weaknesses' continued to undercut efforts to modernize the business environment and reduce bureaucracy. Furthermore, 'trade barriers' and 'burdensome investment regulations' tended to inhibit the development of business and impede the key national strategy of diversifying the economy.

Part of the reason why Angola tended to be among the bottom ten performers in this index was that some investors believed there were many obstacles to setting up and doing business there. As we observed in the case of Ango-Re, the Angolan government had been trying unsuccessfully to establish a national reinsurance company since 2003. The authorities attempted again in 2008 and 2015 without any success, and it was not clear why this was not happening. Although the setting up of a national reinsurer was defined as part of the strategy of the government aimed at securing national interests and promoting local retention of risks in Angola to reduce flight of capital through reinsurance, the project had simply failed to take off. We hoped that the planned future insurance regulatory review, as discussed in Chapter 4, could also look at cases such as this and address the challenge of the bureaucracy, which appeared to be blocking some investments whilst permitting others.

In addition, as we've observed in this book, there were many pieces of legislation in the regulatory framework and numerous reporting requirements. This problem of over-regulation was highlighted as well in the *Africa Insurance Barometer 2017* (AIO, 2017: 39). As observed in this study, the problem was compounded by a lack of resources and technical capacity of the regulatory authority to meaningfully apply the law and ensure financial soundness of the insurance market, as well as ensure consumer protection.

As discussed above, the Angolan government had started reforming some of the regulatory framework for doing business. It appeared that the authorities would continue to make changes aimed at improving the operating environment for business as part of the national strategy to diversify the economy and reduce dependency on revenue from extraction of oil and gas.

# References

Administração Geral Tributária (2017), *Guia do Sistema Tributário Angolano*. Luanda: WhereAngola Book Publisher.

African Insurance Organisation (2017), Africa Insurance Barometer 2017, prepared by Dr Schanz. Zurich: Alms and Company AG.

Deloitte (2017), *Guide to Fiscal Information—Key Economies in Africa*. Johannesburg: Creative Solutions at Deloitte.

Macauhub (2018), 'VAT in Angola Will Initially Be Applied to Large Taxpayers', https://macauhub.com.mo/2018/06/08/pt-iva-em-angola-sera-aplicado-inicialmente-aos-grandes-contribuintes/ (accessed 15 June 2018).

The Heritage Foundation (2018), 'Index of Economic Freedom', https://www.heritage.org/index/pdf/2018/countries/angola.pdf (accessed 25 April 2018).

The World Bank (2017), *Doing Business 2017: Equal Opportunity for All*, 14th ed. Washington, DC: World Bank.

Wasuma, Brian (2017a). 'Price Fixing Was the Lifeline of Insurers, Says Regulator', *Daily Nation*, 5 March 2017, https://www.nation.co.ke/business/price-fixing-saves-insurance-firms/996-3838220-nd3the/index.html (accessed 19 May 2018).

Wasuma, Brian (2017b). *'Regulator Stopped from Fixing Prices of Car Insurance'*, *Business Daily*, 12 April 2017, https://www.businessdailyafrica.com/corporate/IRA-stopped-fixing-price-car-insurance/539550-3886906-ban32sz/index.html (accessed 19 May 2018).

Chapter 12

# FUTURE DEVELOPMENT PROSPECTS

*The difficulty lies not so much in developing new
ideas as in escaping from old ones.*

—*John Maynard Keynes*

We've discussed in this book the emergence of insurance in Angola during
the colonial period. This was followed by a monopoly insurance market
in the period from 1975 up to the beginning of the twenty-first century
when the policymakers started liberalising the insurance market following
key shifts in the political economy of Angola from socialism to market-
based economy. We identified a number of significant achievements by
Angolan policymakers, insurance regulatory authorities, and operators in
the insurance market in this transition period. At the same time, Angola
was also identified as one of the leading seven frontier insurance markets
in Africa with huge potential for growth of insurance if appropriate
development policies were to be implemented.

We also noted that the Angolan authorities themselves acknowledged
that there was still some work to be done to update and develop the
legal framework of insurance business. It was on this basis that the
Angolan policymakers were planning to initiate a comprehensive reform
of insurance legislation. The proposed reforms were part of an emerging
national strategy of improving the operating business environment in the
country and of stimulating growth of non-oil sectors in order to make the
economy less dependent on extractive industries.

Financial services, including insurance activities, were part of the other sectors that the government wanted to see attaining a bigger stake of the national economy. For the insurance sector, this would translate into reduction of the protection gap and an increase of the penetration rate of insurance. We have identified in this book some of the key obstacles to the development of the Angolan insurance market and have recommended solutions as outlined below.

## 12.1 STRIKING THE RIGHT BALANCE IN REGULATION

Insurance regulation was ranked as the most critical factor in influencing development of insurance markets in Africa in the *Africa Insurance Barometer 2017* (AIO, 2017: 47). It was observed in this survey that in most African countries, regulation tended to be the principal 'weakness' and 'threat' to development of the insurance market. In order to create an 'enabling regulatory environment', regulators had to ensure that they strike the right balance in terms of focus and degree of regulation.

We reflected on one of the key contemporary debates: whether the thrust of the regulatory framework should be to protect insurance operators or the consumers. We have observed that insurance regulations in Angola were highly focussed on supporting and protecting the development of insurers and any reinsurers that were supposed to be eventually registered locally. We tended to support the school of thinking that argued that the focus of the regulator was to be mainly on protecting consumers. According to the Africa Insurance Barometer, given that in Africa buyers of insurance still did not trust and had no confidence in insurance, regulators were to focus on protecting the interests of policyholders (AIO, 2017: 47).

As far as degree or level of regulation was concerned, we believed that regulation was supposed to be neither too little nor too much. We had observed that the emerging Angolan insurance regulatory framework aimed clearly for a very high level of rules-based supervision and control supported by an intense regulatory reporting structure. We were of the opinion that overregulation could end up creating challenges for the regulator of technical capacity and resources. At the same time, for the few companies that would try to be fully compliant, the current framework would create major regulatory burdens and costs.

## 12.2 PRICE CONTROLS

Following the transition from a monopoly to an insurance market based on competition from the beginning of the twenty-first century, we observed that one of the major preoccupations of the regulatory authorities had been to control the pricing of insurance. As we discussed in Chapter 9, there were strict requirements on submission to the regulator of premium rates as defined in executive decree no. 58/02 of 5 December 2002. In addition, there were minimum legal rates for some of the classes of business. We were aware that the idea of setting minimum rates was seen as part of an effort to ensure that insurers were charging adequate pricing to cover future liabilities. It was intended to address the problem of undercutting of prices that tended to happen with increased competition. We believed that this was another illustration of situations where the regulator could be overreaching.

We were aware of the importance of safeguarding the financial soundness of the insurance markets. However, we were of the opinion that instead of protectionism and price controls, financial soundness could be more effectively addressed through an appropriate regulatory framework which required insurers to demonstrate proactively how they were managing the risks to which they were exposed and that they had adequate funds to cover their liabilities. In order for such processes as adequate risk pricing to become an effective part of the regulatory framework, the first thing that needed to happen was a 'paradigm shift' in the regulatory model, as we shall discuss in the next recommendation below.

## 12.3 RISK-BASED REGULATORY FRAMEWORK

As we discussed in this book, Angola was still subject to the traditional compliance-based regulatory framework. We believed that there could be an opportunity to shift to the emerging model of risk-based regulatory framework, as discussed in Chapter 3. One of the key issues that would be addressed with this new regulatory model was to link the conditions for capitalisation to the type of business to be underwritten by each insurer as per their specific business-case. We believed that we could start seeing new exploration in some of the neglected areas, such as microinsurance and financial inclusion-related insurance business. We hoped that this would be one of the items covered in the planned insurance policy reform exercise in Angola.

## 12.4 ALIGNMENT OF INSURANCE LEGISLATION WITH NATIONAL DEVELOPMENT POLICIES

We observed in Chapter 5 that the current General Law of Insurance stated a minimum amount of local shareholding required for insurance license applications (ch. III, s. III, art. 22). This was in alignment with the economic development policies at the beginning of the twenty-first century, when the main preoccupation of policymakers was promoting local empowerment of Angolans through minimum quotas of shareholding and regulations aimed at making it difficult to set up a new business unless the majority shareholding was local.

As we discussed in Chapter 11, the Private Investments Law of 2018 removed the requirement of local shareholding. We believed that this was one of the areas requiring attention in the proposed review of the insurance regulatory framework in order to ensure alignment with the new perspectives of the policymakers. It appeared very clear to us that the government wanted to promote more foreign direct investment and was prepared to eliminate barriers to entry for foreign investors.

## 12.5 DEVELOPMENT OF ACTUARIAL SKILLS

As we noted from the interview of the consulting actuary of PwC in Chapter 10, there was a critical lack of actuaries in Angola and most African countries. The implementation of the new regulatory framework as we discussed above would not be feasible in the short- to medium-term due to a lack of actuarial skills that were required to support this model. In addition, actuaries were also a key element in providing technical solutions to the major problem of undercutting of insurance prices. In order to avoid the reliance of insurers on thumb-sucked rates, actuarial skills were essential for purposes of developing a technical basis for pricing of insurance. Without actuarial processes such as 'risk modelling', 'profit testing', 'experience reviews', actuarial reviews, and 'calculation of solvency positions', insurers faced the risk of 'mispricing' and 'miscalculation' of reserves (de Leers and Chow, 2016: 50).

Given the critical value of actuarial skills in insurance, there was a need to design, plan, and implement programmes aimed at development of actuarial skills in Angola and the rest of Africa. We noted efforts of some of the insurance institutes on the continent. We were also aware of meaningful initiatives from the new African Leadership University (ALU).[49] Through a recently established School of Insurance, they hoped to create mechanisms to support and assist students interested in actuarial studies. One of the key reasons why the few students from Africa who enrolled for actuarial fellowship studies tended not to complete their studies was a lack of support and mentorship. As we shall begin to have more actuarial skills in African insurance markets and in the regulatory bodies, there should be an improved level of professionalism in how insurance business is conducted. Elevation of levels of professionalism was one of the key factors to assist in improving soundness of insurance markets.

## 12.6 CONSUMER PROTECTION

We noted that Angola had new legislation aimed at protecting consumers in general. This was a major achievement given the history of the political economy of Angola and the fundamental transformation of the market at the beginning of the twenty-first century. However, there could be further improvements, especially in the areas of formation of effective institutions aimed at defending the rights of consumers. One of the key areas of interest was that of conflict resolution mechanisms, as we shall discuss below.

---

[49] Read more about ALU and their initiatives to support students interested pursuing actuarial studies on their website at https://www.alueducation.com/soi/specialwased-undergraduate-programmes/ (accessed 20 June 2018).

## 12.7 INSURANCE DISPUTE RESOLUTION MECHANISMS

We saw the notable effort of the regulator in Angola in the legislation regarding handling of insurance complaints. However, we also noted that it was not clear how many companies were actually in full compliance. We believed that the internal dispute resolution mechanism would become more effective if supported by an appropriate external mechanism. We would like to refer to examples of autonomous mechanisms such as the offices of the ombudsman in South Africa and in Kenya.

We also believed that an effective mechanism for resolution of insurance disputes was essential in order to restore consumer confidence in insurance (Galgut, 2008: 290). Such entities were to be encouraged to publish appropriate reports identifying any systematic issues affecting the sector. As could be noted in the reports of the insurance ombudsman in South Africa, many of the complaints from consumers were valid cases. We believed that the insurance market did not have to wait for the government to set up such mechanisms. The insurance market could take the initiative of setting up such an entity as some form of self-regulation, as recommended by Lester (2009: 18).

## 12.8 ALIGNMENT WITH THE COMPETITION REGULATION

A key milestone was achieved in the transition of the economic policy framework of Angola from central planning to market-based competition when the lawmakers approved the competition law in the first half of 2018, as discussed in Chapter 11. However, we noted a number of rules and regulations in the insurance legislative framework that appeared to us to be anti-competitive. As mentioned in Chapter 9, for instance, the Regulations on Insurance Rating Guidelines made provisions for fixed premium rates for specified lines of business, prescribed rates of administration fees, and standard insurance wordings. We saw that in South Africa, following application of similar competition legislation, the insurance market found it necessary to stop all practices that could be perceived to violate this regulatory framework, even if they felt that the same activities were supposed to benefit the consumer. We believed that the Angolan policymakers needed to reflect on the same question in the planned reforms of the insurance regulatory framework in order to address some of the contradictions with fundamental principles of competition legislation.

## 12.9 INTERMEDIARIES PREMIUM GUARANTEES

As noted in Chapter 6, there was no mechanism to protect premium funds paid through insurance intermediaries. This was an essential aspect of processes aimed at improving consumer protection by ensuring that buyers of insurance were not prejudiced in the event of mishandling of their premium by intermediaries. We discussed two options for protecting premium funds as follows:

- creation of an Intermediaries Guarantee Fund, such as the model in South Africa
- requirement for intermediaries to arrange insurance or bank guarantees, as per the approach in Portugal

We noted that it would not always be easy to implement in all territories the option of setting up guarantee funds. For countries like Angola where red tape remained a major challenge, the option of an appropriate form of guarantee could be the more practical solution, since it relied on market-led solutions that could be supported by the private financial sector.

## 12.10 UNDERWRITING GUIDELINES FOR OBLIGATORY INSURANCE

In Chapter 7, we identified at least eleven types of obligatory insurance that were supposed to be underwritten by the private insurance market. However, there were no regulations specifying exactly the scope and limit of cover for most of these obligatory types of insurance. As part of the current insurance legislation reform exercises, there could be a process identifying all references to obligatory insurance and seeing where supporting regulations were required in order to improve clarity on the nature and scope of required types of insurance. We should note that the insurance market would need to ensure that it avoided any actions that could be seen as violations of the new competition law.

## 12.11 EASE OF DOING INSURANCE BUSINESS

As we discussed in Chapter 11, in general, Angola tended to rank poorly on global benchmarks for ease of doing business. For insurance business in particular, the current regulatory framework was bureaucratic, and there were major barriers to entry, especially for foreign direct investment. We also noted that there were onerous reporting conditions and very intrusive inspection. We identified more than forty direct insurance-related reporting requirements. In the extreme case of WCA insurance, insurers had to report to six different official entities. For one of the obligatory requirements for this class of business, the insurer was supposed to submit to an appropriate court four copies of an official half-yearly claim notification form requiring completion of eighteen different items for each individual case.

We believed that as part of the planned reform of the insurance regulatory framework, policymakers could address, amongst other things, the complexity of doing insurance business and the need to streamline reporting requirements. We had an impression that the executive legislature, under the leadership of President João Lourenço, was committed to carrying out some of the major changes that were required in order to create a more conducive environment for doing business in general. The Angolan government had identified this as one of the key conditions to attract much-needed foreign direct investment. The reforms included cutting of red tape for setting up and running businesses as well as eliminating rules aimed at imposing local shareholding.

## 12.12 TAXES APPLICABLE TO INSURANCE

We reviewed the basic details of the tax system of Angola in Chapter 11 and identified the types that were supposed to be charged in insurance transactions. We noted that insurance premium was subject to the stamp tax and a levy of the insurance regulator. We believed that it could be useful for the regulatory body to avail, for the benefit of those interested, details on all these taxes. You can find an example of the transparent disclosure of such information on the website of the Portuguese insurance regulatory authority (ASF, 20016b).

## 12.13 MARKET REPORT

We noted that the insurance regulator had issued a market report of good quality. We thought it was a good initiative that the report was compiled with the support of PwC, an independent auditing firm. However, as at the end of the first half of 2018, the most recently published report was for the period 2011–13. We believed that a market report with statistics from five years ago could not be relied on to assess financial soundness of the insurers. We also believed that there was room for improvement in the methodology followed in the report. We would like to note that not all the authorities in Angola could be accused of failing to produce appropriate and timely reports for the benefit of the public. We discussed in Chapter 5 the case of BODIVA, the stock exchange regulatory body that was issuing reports on a regular basis on their area of focus. We also discussed in Chapter 7 the case of the Labour Inspector-General that was publishing up-to-date reports on work-related accidents.

## 12.14 UPDATING OF INFORMATION ON ANGOLA

We have noted that some of the key reports and directories on the insurance business in Angola are outdated. For instance, the *African Insurance Regulatory Directory* (Africa Re, 2015: 41) indicated that there were no restrictions on foreign investments and no compulsory reinsurance. However, in our review in this book, we noted that it was also important for potential investors in this market to be aware of some of the more nuanced details that could potentially affect their initiatives. As we discussed in Chapter 5, there were clearly more onerous obligations and clearance processes if a foreign investor were to plan to set up a wholly owned subsidiary.

Furthermore, in our review of the coinsurance and reinsurance regulations in Chapter 8, we noted that the legislation of Angola actually had provisions for the cession of up to 30 per cent as statutory reinsurance cession to the local reinsurance market. Nonetheless, in almost a decade, the Angolan Government had not completed its ambitious project of setting up of a national reinsurance company. If in the future this were to happen, one could anticipate that there would automatically be a requirement for statutory reinsurance, due to already existing legal conditions that clearly made a provision for such a cession.

## 12.15 OCCUPATIONAL SAFETY HYGIENE AND HEALTH

From the early days of the economic liberalisation process, the lawmakers of Angola passed a progressive piece of legislation regarding occupational safety, hygiene, and health. We believed that this piece of legislation established appropriate principles for the development of appropriate risk management programmes and activities in workplaces. We believed that the local insurance market could take advantage of this legal framework to develop appropriate guidelines on some of the critical risk-related responsibilities of employers. This regulatory framework referred to legal requirements including internal occupational risk regulations, risk inspections, medical examinations, risk-related committees, accidents reporting requirements, training on risk, awareness of occupational risk, and legal penalties for non-compliance.

## 12.16 NON-EXISTENT INSTITUTIONS

The insurance legislative framework made reference to a number of institutions that were critical for the function of the insurance market. We believed that these were notable initiatives. However, it appeared that some of them had not yet been established or were not yet functional. We noted in Chapter 7 that there was supposed to be a National Motor Insurance Data Centre. This would be a useful mechanism to fight the problem of insurance fraud. We also discussed a handful of insurance-related funds in Chapter 4. It was unclear if some of them, such as the Environmental Impairment Fund and Credit Guarantee Fund, were already operational. For the others that were already in place, it appeared that there were concerns regarding accountability, as we shall discuss in the next recommendation.

## 12.17 ACCOUNTABILITY AND SERVICE STANDARDS FOR PUBLIC FUNDS

We would like to begin by acknowledging the efforts of the authorities in trying to create public funds intended to provide protection to consumers. However, we also noted major complaints about lack of delivery of any services from these entities. We believed that the solutions required to address these issues included improved levels of transparency and accountability of the operations of such entities. We looked at the example of the new stock exchange BODIVA that had appropriately issued annual financial accounts. These accounts were a useful mechanism for interested parties to verify their financial soundness. In addition, it was important for Angolan institutions to establish service level agreements like those used for similar public funds in Portugal.[50]

## 12.18 RESEARCH ON LACK OF PENETRATION OF INSURANCE

One of the key recurring themes in this book and other insurance literature that we reviewed was the question of stubbornly low rates of penetration of insurance even for types that were supposed to be obligatory by law. Notwithstanding the efforts of regulators in Angola and other African countries who had gone too far, in our view, in trying to secure and urge people to at least subscribe to the obligatory insurance, there was very little progress. Resistance to obligatory insurance requirements was so strong that in some of African countries, there was an emerging problem of fake insurance. In a study of another frontier insurance market, Nigeria, it was reported that up to 60 per cent of obligatory insurance policies for motor were not genuine insurance cover (PwC, 2015: 6). Many people were prepared to avoid buying insurance by deliberately looking for fake documents so they would not be harassed by enforcement authorities.

We believed that it could be useful for entities such as the African Insurance Organisation (AIO) to commission a research exercise on case studies of successful implementation of obligatory types of insurance. We were aware that some models had been very effective in some insurance markets, even in Africa. The AIO could follow the same approach as applied in the study on the issue of flight of capital from African insurance markets through 'unnecessary' transfers (PwC, 2016).

---

[50] The claims procedures on the website of ASF contain clear timelines for execution of required steps from the beginning to the end of the claim process: http://www. asf.com.pt/NR/rdonlyres/FA5AE36D-E3C5-4BF4-8CFA-0E9301895D58/0/ Circuito_Processo_Sinistros.pdf (accessed 25 May 2018).

## 12.19 CASE STUDY ON HANDLING OF OIL AND GAS BUSINESS

There was a lot of debate in Angola on what was supposed to be the right model for promoting local retention and skills development in the local insurance market, in alignment with the stated goals of the policymakers. We agreed with the observation at the 2018 Oil and Gas Forum that the current model of one leader handling all the underwriting did not permit transfer of knowledge to all the key stakeholders in the obligatory coinsurance. We were also aware that there were similar debates in Mozambique following the recent major gas explorations there. We believed that Angola, Mozambique, and many other African countries could benefit from a case study on some of the successful models on development of local capacity and skills. We believed that there were useful lessons to learn from some of the more collaborative models that had been implemented in countries like Uganda.

## 12.20 REVIEW OF THE INSURANCE REGULATORY FRAMEWORK

Fortuitously, as we were preparing to publish this case study, we noted the initiative by Angolan policymakers to reform the insurance legislative framework. We hoped that through our efforts in this book, we could make a few meaningful contributions to discussions on the key questions affecting development of insurance in Angola. We did not doubt the good intentions of lawmakers in aiming to modernise the insurance regulatory framework in alignment with emerging key global standards. However, we believed that the reform process was also an opportunity to resolve some of the pre-existing issues relating to the local context of the development of insurance in this market, as we have presented in this case study of the development of insurance in Angola. We believed that the rules and regulations for doing insurance business could be reviewed in order to create a conducive business environment for improvement of performance in this frontier insurance market and for the attainment of the highly desired goal of increased penetration of insurance.

*To improve was to change; to be perfect was to*
*change often.—Winston Churchill*

# References

Africa Re (2015), *The African Insurance Regulatory Directory*, analysis prepared by Dr Schanz, Zurich: Alms and Company AG.

African Insurance Organisation (2017). *Africa Insurance Barometer 2017*, prepared by Dr Schanz. Zurich: Alms and Company AG.

ASF (2016), 'Taxas parafiscais e fiscais', as published on the website of ASF, 20 June 2016, http://www.asf.com.pt/NR/rdonlyres/DF89C51A-D76D-4291-BE35-8D23D7C6F430/0/taxas.pdf (accessed 20 May 2018).

de Leers, Renata, and Queenie Chow (2016), 'Pricing challenges in Africa', *African Insurance Bulletin*, vol. 007, May 2016.

Galgut, B. (2008), 'Promoting public confidence in the industry', Content, vol. 20, no. 11, April 2008. Randburg: Cover Publications, 29–30.

Lester, Rodney (2009), 'Consumer Protection Insurance', *Primer Series on Insurance*, Issue 7, August 2009. Washington: The World Bank.

PwC (2015), 'Africa Insurance Trends: Strategic and Emerging Trends in Insurance Markets in Nigeria', https://www.pwc.com/ng/en/assets/pdf/nigeria-insurance-survey.pdf (accessed 25 May 2018).

PwC (2016), 'African Insurance Organisation Study on the Transfer of Insurance Premiums Offshore', http://www.african-insurance.org/documents/2016%20AIO%20Executive%20summary_Final%20-%20English.pdf (accessed 25 May 2018).

Swiss Re (2016), 'Insuring the Frontier Markets', *Sigma*, no. 2/2016. Zurich: Swiss Reinsurance Company Ltd.

# Bibliography

Achega, Gonçalo, *Legislação de Mercados Financeiros: Direito Bancário e dos Seguros* (Luanda, 2014).

Administração Geral Tributária, *Guia do Sistema Tributário Angolano* (Luanda, 2017).

Africa Re, *The African Insurance Regulation Directory*, prepared by Dr Schanz (Zurich, 2015).

African Insurance Organisation, *Africa Insurance Barometer 2017*, prepared by Dr Schanz (Zurich, 2017).

African Reinsurance Corporation, *Establishment Agreement of the African Reinsurance Corporation of 24 February 1976* (1976).

AngoNotícias, 'ENSA Lança Seguro Agrícola', *Jornal Mercado*, 27 June 2018, http://www.angonoticias.com/Artigos/item/58316/ensa-lanca-seguro-agricola (accessed 30 June 2018).

AngoNotícias, 'Seguros: Regulador diz que não há risco de falência', 14 April 2018, http://www.angonoticias.com/Artigos/item/57664/seguros-regulador-diz-que-nao-ha-risco-de-falencia.

Angop, 'Angola Stock Exchange May Play Strategic Role in SADC', http://www.angop.ao/angola/en_us/noticias/economia/2017/2/11/Angola-Stock-Exchange-may-play-strategic-role-SADC, f9423b85-4a9c-4008-951a-0674cb75d222.html (accessed 11 May 2018).

ARSEG, *Desafios e Oportunidades: Estudo sobre o Sector Segurador e dos Fundos de Pensões em Angola* (Angola, 2015).

ARSEG, *Fundo de Actualização e Regularização de Seguros (FUNSEG)*, http://www.arseg.ao/index.php?option=com_content&view=article&id=127&Itemid=180&lang=pt (accessed 16 May 2018).

ARSEG, *Fundo de Garantia Automóvel (FGA)*, http://www.arseg.ao/index. php?option=com_content&view=article&id=137&Itemid=175&lang= pt (accessed 15 May 2018).

ASF, *Relatório do Setor Segurador e dos Fundos de Pensões*, http://www.asf. com.pt/NR/exeres/9761BAC3-D3A7-4DEB-928C-C1FAAB73D544. htm (accessed 26 April 2018).

ASF, 'Taxas parafiscais e fiscais', http://www.asf.com.pt/NR/rdonlyres/ DF89C51A-D76D-4291-BE35-8D23D7C6F430/0/taxas.pdf (accessed 20 May 2018).

AXCO, *Angola: Non-Life Insurance Market Report* (London, 2011).

AXCO, *Angola: Non-Life Insurance Market Report* (London, 2018).

Bermuda Monetary Authority, 'AAA Reinsurance Limited: 2016 Financial Statements', http://www.bma.bm/Insurance/CURRENT%20 FULL%20FILINGS%20CLASS%203A/AAA%20Reinsurance%20 Limited%20-%202016%20Financial%20Statements.pdf (accessed 8 May 2018).

Bernstein, P. L., *Against the Gods: the Remarkable Story of Risk* (New York, 1996).

BODIVA, 'Relatório e Contas 2015', http://www.bodiva.ao/files/relatorio-contas/relatorio-e-contas-2015.pdf (accessed 11 May 2018).

Bordalo, Ricardo, 'FMI e Governo Definem Metas para a Assistência Técnica a Angola' *Novo Jornal*, http://www.novojornal.co.ao/economia/interior/ fmi-e-governo-definem-metas-para-a-assistencia-tecnica-a-angola---medidas-severas-em-perspectiva-57174.html?utm_term=Bom+dia% 2C+sim.+-+Newsletter+Novo+Jornal&utm_campaign=Newsletters &utm_source=e-goi&utm_medium=email (accessed on 6 August 2018).

Borscheid, Peter, 'Global Insurance Networks', in Harold James, ed., *The Value of Risk: Swiss Re and the History of Reinsurance* (New York: 2013), 23–105.

Carmichael, J. and Pormerleano, M., *The Development and Regulation of Non-Banking Financial Institutions* (Washington: 2002).

Ciecka, James, E., 'Edmond's Life Table and Its Uses', *Journal of Legal Economics*, 15/1 (2008), 65–74.

Correia, Raquel Almeida, 'Ao fim nove anos, a angolana TAAG volta a sobrevoar a Europa', *Público* (2016), https://www.publico.pt/2016/06/10/

economia/noticia/ao-fim-nove-anos-a-angolana-taag-volta-a-sobrevoar-o-ceu-da-europa-1734748 (accessed 20 May 2018).

da Conceião, Alcino Izata, *Angola no Contexto Financeiro Global* (Luanda, 2016).

da Silva, Valter Felipe Duarte, *O Banco Nacional de Angola e a Crise Financeira* (Luanda, 2012).

de Abreu, Ana Edith Viegas, *100 Anos de Legislação de Seguros em Angola* (Luanda, 2014).

de Leers, Renata, and Chow, Queenie, 'Pricing challenges in Africa', *African Insurance Bulletin*, 7, May 2016.

da Rocha, Alves, 'Economic Growth in Angola to 2017 – The Main Challenges', Angola Brief, December 2012, vol. 2 no. 4, Centro de Estudo e a Investigação Científica – Universidade Católica de Angola & CMI (2012)

Deloitte, *Guide to Fiscal Information: Key Economies in Africa* (Johannesburg, 2017).

Demirgüç-Kunt, Asli, Karacaovali, Baybars, and Laeven, Luc. 'Deposit Insurance around the World: A Comprehensive Database', World Bank (2005), http://siteresources. worldbank.org/INTRES/Resources/469232-1107449512766/ DepositInsuranceDatabasePaper_DKL.pdf (accessed 16 April 2018).

*Diário da República Electrónica*, decreto-lei 44702, de 17 de Novembro, https://dre.tretas.org/dre/259938/decreto-lei-44702-de-17-de-novembro (accessed on 20 May 2018).

Dias, Nélia Daniel, *Legislação Financeira e dos Seguros* (Luanda, 2012).

Dludla, Nqobile, and Abdennebi, Zakia, 'Sanlam Buys out Morocco's SAHAM Finances in $1 Billion Africa Expansion', *Reuters* (2018), https://www.reuters.com/article/us-sanlam-semil-stake/sanlam-buys-out-moroccos-saham-finances-in-1-billion-african-expansion-idUSKCN1GK0LJ (accessed on 15 June 2018).

EY, *Sub-Saharan Africa: The Evolution of Insurance Regulation* (London: 2016).

FA News, 'No winners as Multimark III disappears' (2007), https://www. fanews.co.za/article/magazine-archives-fanews-fanuus/60/short-term/1317/no-winners-as-multimark-iii-disappears/10008 (accessed on 5 June 2018).

Ferreira, Manuel Ennes, *Angola: Conflict and Development, 1961-2002*, *Economics of Peace and Security Journal*, 1 (2006), www.epsjournal. org.uk.

Ferreira, Monteiro Rolando, 'Como e Seguro Nasceu', *Seguros*: Série Técnica, 114, December 1966, 121–123 (Lisboa: 1966).

Fitch Ratings, 'Fitch Revises Nova Sociedade de Seguros de Angola's Outlook to Stable; Affirms IFS at "B"' (2018), https://www.fitchratings. com/site/pr/10029450 (accessed 28 May 2018).

FocusEconomics, 'Angola Economic Outlook', 20 March 2018, https:// www.focus-economics.com/countries/angola.

Galgut, B., 'Promoting public confidence in the industry', *Content*, 20/11 (Randburg, 2008).

Governo de Angola, 'Regulamento das Organizações Não Governamentais', http://www.governo.gov.ao/VerLegislacao.aspx?id=777 (accessed 15 May 2018).

Hafeman, Michael, *The Role of the Actuary in Insurance*, Primer Series on Insurance, Issue 4, May 2009 (Washington, 2009).

Hebo, Quingila, 'Das 26 seguradoras licenciadas 19 podem fechar brevemente', *Expansão*, 9 February 2018.

Hossi, Emerson, 'Fórum Segurador Oil & Gas Debate Repartição do Know-How Técnico no Sector Petrolífero', *Notícias de Angola*, https://www.noticiasdeangola.co.ao/forum-segurador-oilgas-debate-reparticao-do-know-how-tecnico-no-sector-petrolifero/ (accessed 15 June 2018).

IAIS, 'Members', https://www.iawasweb.org/page/about-the-iawas/iawas-members (accessed 20 May 2018).

IISA, 'Principles of Short Term Insurance', Insurance Institute of South Africa (2011).

Insurance Guarantee Fund, http://www.igfsec45.co.za/#!/ (accessed on 29 June 2018).

International Maritime Organization, 'International Convention on Civil Liability for Oil Pollution Damage', http://www.imo.org/en/About/conventions/listofconventions/pages/international-convention-on-civil-liability-for-oil-pollution-damage-(clc).aspx (accessed 15 June 2018).

Irukwu, J. O. *Fundamentals of Insurance Law* (London, 2007).

Irukwu, J. O. *Insurance Management in Africa* (Lagos, 1998).

KPMG, *Review of the Insurance and Pension Fund Sector in Angola* (Luanda, 2012).

Leiria, Manuel, *Marketing de Seguros* (Lisboa, 2013).

Lester, Rodney, *Consumer Protection Insurance*, Primer Series on Insurance, Issue 7, August 2009 (Washington, 2009).

LexLink, 'Lei da Concorrência', Lei 5/18 de 10 de Maio (2009), https://www.lexlink.eu/FileGet.aspx?FileId=3007948 (accessed 17 May 2018).

Macauhub, 'Angola: TAAG prepares for evaluation and hopes to re-launch flights to Europe in July' (2009), https://macauhub.com.mo/2009/03/05/6664/ (accessed 20 May 2018).

Macauhub, 'Angolan airline TAAG removed from EU blacklist', 14 June 2016, https://macauhub.com.mo/2016/06/14/angolan-airline-taag-removed-from-eu-blacklist/ (accessed 20 May 2018).

Macauhub, 'Angola's National Reinsurance Company Starts Operating in 2018', https://macauhub.com.mo/2018/06/07/pt-empresa-nacional-de-resseguros-de-angola-comeca-a-funcionar-em-2018/ (accessed 15 June 2018).

Macauhub, 'VAT in Angola will initially be applied to large taxpayers,' https://macauhub.com.mo/2018/06/08/pt-iva-em-angola-sera-aplicado-inicialmente-aos-grandes-contribuintes/ (accessed 15 June 2018).

Mathonsi, George, 'Cobrança e Canalização de Prémios às Seguradoras', paper presented at the Insurance Seminar of the ISSM (2013).

McCord, Michael J., 'The Partner-Agent Model: Challenges and Opportunities', in Churchill, Craig, ed., *Protecting the Poor: A Microinsurance Compendium* (Geneva, 2008), 357–377.

Mehr, Robert, I., and Cammack, Emerson, *Principles of Insurance* (Illinois, 1972).

Muchena, Israel, *Development of Insurance in Mozambique* (Bloomington, 2018).

Muchena, Israel, 'The Mozambican Insurance Market', in *The African Reinsurer* 26 (Lagos, 2012), 32–35.

Mumenthaler, C., 'Open Markets: The Key to Enhancing Societal Resilience', in *Reactions CEO Risk Forum* (London, 2017).

Muzima, Joel, and Galardo, Glenda, 'Country Notes: Angola 2017', in *African Economic Outlook* 2017, AfDB, OECD, and UNDP.

Naik, Dhirendra Narayan, 'Social Security and Social Insurance' in *Journal of Civil and Legal Sciences* 5/5 (2016), https://www.omicsonline.org/ open-access/social-security-and-social-insurance-2169-0170-1000206. pdf (accessed 28 May 2018).

Nascimento, Luís, 'História do Seguro,' 4 November 2015, http:// hwastoriadoseguro.com/sobre/ (accessed on 20 May 2018).

Nazaré, Domingas Miguel, *A ENSA e a Reforma do Sector Seguradora em Angola* (Luanda, 2008).

NOSSA, 'Relatório e Contas Anual 2017', http://www.nossaseguros.ao/ uploads/ widgets/20/201812281542515c26447be432b.pdf [Accessed 26 March 2019]

Novo Jornal, 'Nove mortes em 666 acidentes de trabalho registados em Angola no primeiro semestre de 2018', http://www.novojornal.co.ao/ sociedade/interior/nove-mortes-em-666-acidentes-de-trabalho-regwastados-em-angola-no-primeiro-semestre-de-2018-57140.html? utm_term=Bom+dia%2C+sim.+-+Newsletter+Novo+Jornal&utm_ campaign=Newsletters&utm_source=e-goi&utm_medium=email (accessed 1 August 2018).

Novo Jornal, 'Primeira consequência da chegada do FMI foi no "rating" do pais, Fitch passa Angola de perspectiva negativa para estável', 26 April 2018, http://www.novojornal.co.ao/economia/interior/primeira-consequencia-da-chegada-do-fmi-foi-no-rating-do-pawas-fitch-passa-angola-de-perspectiva-negativa-para-estavel-52890.html?utm_term= Bom+dia%2C+sim.+-+Newsletter+Novo+Jornal&utm_campaign= Newsletters&utm_source=e-goi&utm_medium=email.

Novo Jornal, 'Segurança Social: Apenas 1,7 dos 7,5 Milhões de Trabalhadores Estão Inscritos', http://www.novojornal.co.ao/sociedade/ interior/seguranca-social-apenas-17-dos-75-milhoes-de-trabalhadores-estao-inscritos-57493.html?utm_term=Bom+dia%2C+sim.+- +Newsletter+Novo+Jornal&utm_campaign=Newsletters& utm_source=e-goi&utm_medium=email (accessed 26 August 2018).

OSTI, *The Ombudsman's Briefcase Newsletter*, March 2016, 1, The Ombudsman for Short-Term Insurance, https://www.masthead.co.za/ wp-content/uploads/2016/04/OSTI-Briefcase-Newsletter-1-2016-1. pdf (accessed 15 June 2018).

Pinto, Domingos, 'O Seguro proporciona "paz de espírito", bem-haja o 05 de Agosto', *Club-K Angola*, 8 August 2017, http://www.club-k.net/index.php?option=com_content&view=article&id=28925:o-seguro-proporciona-paz-de-espirito-bem-haja-o-05-de-agosto-domingos-pinto&catid=17&lang=pt&Itemid=1067 (accessed on 20 May 2018).

Portugal, Luís, *Gestão de Seguros Não-Vida* (Lisboa, 2007).

Prudential Insurance Company of America, *The Documentary History of Insurance 1000 BC–1875 AD* (Newark, 1915).

PwC, 'Africa Insurance Trends: Strategic and Emerging Trends in Insurance Markets in Nigeria' (2015), https://www.pwc.com/ng/en/assets/pdf/nigeria-insurance-survey.pdf (accessed 25 May 2018).

PwC, 'African Insurance Organisation Study on the Transfer of Insurance Premiums Offshore' (2016), http://www.african-insurance.org/documents/2016%20AIO%20Executive%20summary_Final%20-%20English.pdf (accessed 25 May 2018).

Rainha, Paula, 'Republic of Angola: Legal System and Research', GlobaLex (2007), http://www.nyulawglobal.org/globalex/Angola.html (accessed 12 April 2018).

Reader, J., *Africa: A Biography of the Continent* (London, 1998).

Secovnie, Robert, 'History of Insurance,' Insurance Training Institute, http://iti-ny.com/H%20wastory%20of%20Insurance%2011-1-16%20wpf%20(13)/HistoryofInsurance.pdf (accessed on 25 June 2018).

Shillington, K., *History of Africa* (New York, 2005).

Silva, Victor, 'Fundo de Garantia Automóvel Angolano é um Fiasco', *Jornal de Angola* (2018), http://jornaldeangola.sapo.ao/opiniao/fundo_de_garantia_automovel__angolano_e_um_fiasco (accessed 18 May 2018).

Sousa, Rosimaria, 'Primeira Academia de Seguros Abre Portas', *Mercado* (2018), http://www.mercado.co.ao/capital-humano/upgrade/jack-ma-timoneiro-do-e-commerce/ (accessed 20 May 2018).

Swiss Re, 'Bancassurance: Emerging Trends, Opportunities and Challenges', *Sigma* 5/2007.

Swiss Re, 'Insuring the Frontier Markets,' *Sigma* 2/2016.

Swiss Re, 'World Insurance in 2015', *Sigma* 3/2016.

The Economist Intelligence Unit, 'BODIVA Plans 2016 Listings', http://country.eiu.com/article.aspx?articleid=503405434&Country=

Angola&topic=Economy&subtopic=Forecast&subsubtopic=Policy+ trends&u=1&pid=1961778780&oid=1961778780 (accessed 11 May 2018).

The Heritage Foundation, 'Index of Economic Freedom', 25 April 2018, https://www.heritage.org/index/pdf/2018/countries/angola.pdf.

The World Bank, *Doing Business 2017: Equal Opportunity for All*, 14th ed. (Washington, DC, 2017).

Thompson, Barineka, 'Promoting the Adoption of Risk-Based Capital in African Insurance Markets', *African Insurance Bulletin* 7, May 2016.

UN, 'Graduation of Angola from the Least Developed Country Category', UN General Assembly Resolution A/RES/70/253, adopted 12 February 2016.

UNDP, *Human Development Indices and Indicators: 2018 Statistical Upgrade* (New York, 2018).

Vasques, José, *Contrato de Seguro* (Coimbra, 1999).

Vaughan, Emmet J., *Fundamentals of Risk and Insurance*, 6th ed. (New York, 1992).

Vivian, Robert W., and Morgan, Jim, *Morgan's History of the Insurance Institute Movement in South Africa* (Cape Town, 2001).

Warner, Rachel, 'Historical Setting', in Collelo, Thomas, ed., *Angola: A Country Study* (Washington, 1991), 5–50.

Wasuma, Brian, 'Price Fixing Was the Lifeline of Insurers, Says Regulator', *Daily Nation*, Sunday, 5 March 2017, https://www.nation.co.ke/ business/price-fixing-saves-insurance-firms/996-3838220-nd3the/ index.html (accessed 19 May 2018).

Wasuma, Brian, 'Regulator Stopped from Fixing Prices of Car Insurance', in *Business Daily*, Wednesday, 12 April 2017, https://www.businessdailyafrica. com/corporate/IRA-stopped-fixing-price-car-insurance/539550- 3886906-ban32sz/index.html (accessed 19 May 2018).

Waty, Teodoro, A... *Direito de Seguros* (Maputo, 2007).

# Appendix I: Licensed Insurers as of the End of 2018

| NO. | NAME OF INSURER | TYPE OF LICENSE | YEAR ESTABLISHED |
|-----|-----------------|-----------------|------------------|
| 1 | ENSA Seguros de Angola, SA | Life, Non-Life | 1978 |
| 2 | AAA Seguros, SA | Life, Non-Life | 2001 |
| 3 | NOSSA Seguros, SA | Life, Non-Life | 2005 |
| 4 | Saham Angola Seguros, SA (formerly GA Angola Seguros) | Life, Non-Life | 2005 |
| 5 | A Mundial Seguros, SA | Life, Non-Life | 2006 |
| 6 | Global Seguros, SA | Life, Non-Life | 2006 |
| 7 | Garantia Seguros, SA | Life, Non-Life | 2008 |
| 8 | Fidelidade Angola Seguros, SA (formerly Universal Seguros) | Life, Non-Life | 2010 |
| 9 | Confiança Seguros, SA | Life, Non-Life | 2010 |
| 10 | Tranquilidade–Corporação Angolana de Seguros, SA | Life, Non-Life | 2010 |
| 11 | Triunfal Seguros | Life, Non-Life | 2011 |
| 12 | Mandume Seguros, SA | Life, Non-Life | 2012 |
| 13 | Protteja Seguros, SA | Life, Non-Life | 2012 |
| 14 | Super Seguros, SA | Life, Non-Life | 2012 |
| 15 | Prudencial Seguros, SA | Life, Non-Life | 2013 |
| 16 | BONWS Seguros, SA | Life, Non-Life | 2014 |
| 17 | BIC Seguros, SA | Life, Non-Life | 2014 |
| 18 | Liberty and Trevo (Angola) Companhia de Seguros, SA | Life, Non-Life | 2015 |
| 19 | Providência Royal Seguros, SA | Life, Non-Life | 2016 |
| 20 | Fortaleza Segura Companhia de Seguros | Life, Non-Life | 2016 |
| 21 | Glinn Seguros, SA | Life, Non-Life | 2016 |
| 22 | STAS–Sociedade Transnacional Angolana de Seguros, SA | Life, Non-Life | 2016 |
| 23 | Master Seguros | Life, Non-Life | 2016 |

| 24 | Sol Seguros | Life, Non-Life | 2016 |
|----|-------------|---------------|------|
| 25 | Aliança Seguros | Life, Non-Life | 2017 |
| 26 | Giant Magic Seguros | Life, Non-Life | 2018 |
| 27 | Internacional Seguros | Life, Non-Life | 2018 |

Source: Website of ARSEG, the Insurance Regulator: http://www.arseg.ao/index.php?option=com_content&view=article&id=123&Itemid=165&lang=pt [Accessed 30 Nov 2018]

# Appendix II: Insurance Companies in Angola in 1974

1.  Alliance Assurance
2.  Commercial Union
3.  Companhia de Seguros A Nacional de Angola
4.  Companhia de Seguros Angolana
5.  Companhia de Seguros Atlas
6.  Companhia de Seguros Bonança
7.  Companhia de Seguros Comércio e Indústria
8.  Companhia de Seguros Confiança e Mundial
9.  Companhia de Seguros Douro
10. Companhia Seguros Garantia África
11. Companhia de Seguros Fidelidade Atlântica
12. Companhia de Seguros Império
13. Companhia de Seguros l'Urbaine Vie
14. Companhia de Seguros o Alentejo
15. Companhia de Seguros o Trabalho
16. Companhia de Seguros Ourique
17. Companhia de Seguros Portugal Previdente
18. Companhia de Seguros Tagus
19. Companhia de Seguros Tranquilidade
20. Companhia de Seguros Ultramarina
21. Companhia de Seguros Universal de Angola
22. Mútua dos Industriais de Pesca
23. Phoenix Assurance Company
24. Sociedade Portuguesa de Seguros

Source: Nazaré (2008: 167) and de Abreu (2014: 27-30)

# Appendix III: Insurance Legal Framework as of the End of 2018

1. Commercial Code as per the Law of 28 June 1888
2. Resolution no. 10/91 of 18 May 1991
   Approval for the Republic of Angola to join the Establishment Agreement of the African Reinsurance Corporation
3. Resolution no. 10/91 of 18 May 1991
   Approval for the Republic of Angola to join the Establishment Agreement of the African Reinsurance Corporation
4. Decree no. 25/98 of 7 August 1998
   Regulation of Pension Funds
5. Decree no. 1/99 of 12 March 1999
   Legal Framework of Mutual Associations
6. Law no. 1/00 of 3 February 2000
   The General Law of Insurance
7. Decree no. 6/ 01 of 2 March 2001
   Reinsurance and Coinsurance Regulations
8. Decree no. 39/01 of 22 June 2001
   Regulations of the Risk Management of Petroleum Operations
9. Decree no. 2/02 of 11 February 2002
   Insurance Contract Regulations
10. Decree no. 7/02 of 9 April 2002
    Transgressions of Insurance Legislation and Sanctions Regime
11. Decree no. 79-A/02 of 5 December 2002
    Chart of Accounts for Insurance Companies
12. Executive decree no. 58/02 of 5 December 2002

Guidelines on Insurance Rating Systems, which we shall simply refer to in this book as *rating guidelines*

13. Executive decree no. 5/03 of 24 January 2003
Regulations on Conditions of Access and Conduct of Business of Insurers

14. Executive decree no. 6/03 of 24 January 2003
Financial Guarantees Regulations

15. Executive decree no. 7/03 of 24 January 2003
Regulations of Insurance Intermediaries

16. Decree no. 9/03 of 21 February 2003
Regulations on the Calculation of the Solvency Margin and Setting up of a Guarantee Fund.

17. Executive decree no. 16/03 of 21 February 2003
Operating Rules for Pension Fund Administration Companies

18. Decree no. 96/04 of 17 December 2004
Establishment of the Insurance Guarantee Fund (FUNSEG)

19. Rectification notice no. 9 of 21 January 2005
Rectification of Decree no. 9/03 of 21 February 2003

20. Decree no. 53/05 of 15 August 2005
Workmen's Compensation Act Insurance Legal Framework

21. Executive decree no. 66/05 of 29 June 2005
Regulations of the Insurance and Pensions Technical Council

22. Joint executive decree of ministries of finance and transport no. 52/05 of 9 May 2005
Exceptional Assumption by the Angolan State of Aviation War and Terrorism Risks up to US$1 billion in excess of US$50 million limit of liability cap from international insurance markets

23. Executive decree no. 70/06 of 7 June 2006
Revision of Minimum Capital Requirements for Insurance Companies

24. Executive decree no. 74/07 of 29 June 2007
Regulations to Streamline the Current Conditions for Accessing and Operating in the Insurance Market

25. Decree 9/09 of 3 June 2009
Rules and Regulations for Air Transportation of Passengers, Baggage and Cargo

26. Decree no. 10/09 of 13 July, 2009

Establishment of the Motor Liability Guarantee Fund

27. Decree no. 35/09 of 11 August 2009
Obligatory Motor Third Party Liability Insurance Regulations

28. Resolution no. 115/09 of 18 December 2009
Resolution in respect of Obligatory Aviation Liability Insurance

29. Circular no. 01/ISS/MF/10 of 2 March 2010
Directive on Rejected Motor Third Party Liability Insurance

30. Circular no. 01/FGA/10 of 26 April 2010
Functions of the Motor Guarantee Fund

31. Circular no. 02/ISS/MF/10 of 1 July 2010
Required Formats of Obligatory Periodical Reports from Insurance Companies to the Regulator

32. Circular no. 03/ISS/MF/10 of 2 August 2010
Directive on Required Formats of Obligatory Periodical Reports from Pensions Funds to the Insurance Regulator

33. Circular no. 04/ISS/MF/10 of 2 August 2010
Directive for pensions fund administrators and insurers that administer pension funds to define the investment policies for funds under their control

34. Circular no. 05/ISS/MF/10 on 2 August 2010
Insurers were instructed to set up guarantees in favour of the Insurance Public Guarantee Fund to serve as collateral for value of assets held to cover insurance reserves

35. Circular no. 06/ISS.MF/10 of 2 August 2010 on insurance intermediation

36. Executive decree no. 179/11 of 2011
Obligatory Provisions for Payment of Premium for Insurance of Workmen's Compensation and Occupational Illnesses

37. Executive decree no. 141/13 of 27 September 2013
Establishment of the new autonomous insurance regulatory body, Agência Angolana de Regulação e Supervisão de Seguros (ARSEG)

38. Circular no. 30/GAPCAARSEG/14 of 5 August 2014
Directive on Reports of Suspicious Operations and Identification of Designated Persons as part of the requirements from the Anti-Money Laundering and Combating of Financing of Terrorism Law

39. Notice no. 1/15 of 13 October of 2015

Establishment of rules and procedures to be followed in the handling of complaints lodged by policyholders, insured parties, beneficiaries, and injured third parties to insurance companies and pension fund administration companies

40. Notice no. 2/15 of 29 December 2015

Regulations on identification and due diligence as well as establishment of a programme of action on anti-money laundering and combating of financing of terrorism, including setting up of the compliance officer in the Organogramme of the entities addressed in this notice.

41. Financial Institutions Law no. 12/2015 of 17 June 2015

42. Presidential order no. 39/16 of 30 March 2016

Designation of ENSA as the Leader of the Coinsurance of Petroleum Activities

43. Presidential decree no. 226/16 of 17 November 2016

Obligatory Aviation Liability Insurance Regulations

44. Executive decree no. 464/16 of 1 December 2016

Update of Fines in Respect of Infringement of the Insurance Law

45. Executive decree no. 465/16 of 1 December 2016

Update of Fines for Infringement of the Regulations Relating to Insurance Intermediaries

46. Presidential legislative decree no. 1/17 of 20 June 2017

Legal regime in respect of Financial Information Tax Reporting in Compliance with the Foreign Account Tax Account Compliance Act (FATCA) of the USA

47. Decree no. 87/18 of 23 March 2018

Establishment of a Taskforce for the Review and Proposal of Reform of the Legal Framework for Insurance and Pensions Business

# Appendix IV: Obligatory Reporting Conditions for Insurers

| Reporting Requirements | Reporting Periods | Legislation |
|---|---|---|
| 1. Special registration with the insurance regulator | Before commencement of operations | Law no. 1/00 of 3 February 2000 (ch. III, s. II, sub-s. II, art. 18) |
| 2. Notification of any changes of registration details | Within 30 days after occurrence of change | Law no. 1/00 of 3 February 2000 (ch. III, s. II, sub-s. II, art. 19) |
| 3. Opening balance statements and report on adjustments in initial business plan | At time of beginning operations within 6 months of registration | Law no. 1/00 of 3 February 2000 (ch. III, s. II, sub-s. III, art. 20) |
| 4. Audited annual accounts as of 31 December and in accordance with the required chart of accounts | 31 March of each year for the immediate previous financial year (the circular from the regulator gives timeline of 30 April) | Law no. 1/00 of 3 February 2000 (ch. III, s. II, sub-s. IV, art. 37, Cl. 1) and circular no. 02/ISS/MF/10 of 1 July 2010 (ch. II, art. 2) |
| 5. All proposed changes of corporate name, capital, mergers, demergers, transfer of majority shareholding, or portfolio transfer from one entity to another | Prior clearance by the regulator whenever this may be required | Law no. 1/00 of 3 February 2000 (ch. III, s. IV, sub-s. IV, art. 37, cl. 1) |
| 6. Application for clearance of transfer abroad of reinsurance or retrocession transactions | Prior clearance by the Central Bank of Angola | Decree no. 6/01 of 2 March 2001 (ch. I, art. 7, cl. 1) |
| 7. Preliminary clearance of planned transfers for annual treaty programmes | Insurance regulator was required to respond within 5 working days | Decree no. 6/01 of 2 March 2001 (ch. I, art. 7, cl. 3) |
| 8. Submission of reinsurance agreements and technical reinsurance cessions reports | Quarterly and consolidated annual report as required by insurance regulator | Decree no. 6/01 of 2 March 2001 (ch. I, art. 10) |
| 9. Duty to appear in the event of notification by the regulator of a violation of rules and regulations of the insurance legislation | Maximum of 5 days to present justification in the event of failure to appear | Decree no. 7/02 of 9 April 2002 (ch. VI, s. I, art. 18, cl. 1) |

| | | |
|---|---|---|
| 10. Payment of a fine for failure to appear after notification from the regulator | Within 15 days | Decree no. 7/02 of 9 April 2002 (ch. VI, s. I, art. 18, cl. 2) |
| 11. Submission of defence in the event of notification of a sanction | Between 10 and 30 days as per notification | Decree no. 7/02 of 9 April 2002 (ch. VI, s. I, art. 19, cl. 3) |
| 12. Notification of cancellation of WCA Insurance to the Social Security regulatory body | As and when this procedure was executed | Executive decree no. 5/03 of 24 January 2003 (ch. VI, art. 30, cl. 1) |
| 13. Declaration of declined risks to the insurance regulator | As and when this occurs | Executive decree no. 5/03 of 24 January 2003 (ch. VII, art. 32, cl. 2) |
| 14. Submission of copies of all intermediation agreements | As and when this occurs | Executive Decree no. 7/03 of 24 January 2003 (ch. I, art. 3, cl. 5) |
| 15. Registration of tied agents through the insurer | As and when clearance was required | Executive decree no. 7/03 of 24 January 2003 (ch. II, art. 5, cl. 1) |
| 16. Submission of proposals for the regulator's qualification tests of individual agents | As and when required | Executive decree no. 7/03 of 24 January 2003 (ch. III, s. I, art. 11, cl. 4) |
| 17. Registration of current table of commissions for insurance intermediaries | Not specified | Executive decree no. 7/03 of 24 January 2003 (ch. VII, art. 28, cl. 3) |
| 18. Application for authorisation to invest in shares and bonds abroad for life insurance funds | Prior clearance required as and when this may be considered | Executive decree no. 5/03 of 24 January 2003 (ch. IV, s. I, art. 11, cl. 2) |
| 19. Submission of receivable premium provision | Up to 30 April of each year for the previous financial year | Executive decree no. 5/03 of 24 January 2003 (ch. IV, art. 28) |
| 20. Notification to the Social Security regulatory body of cancellation of any WCA insurance policy | As and when this occurs | Executive decree no. 5/03 of 24 January 2003 (ch. IV, art. 30) |
| 21. Application for clearance to calculate unexpired risks reserves on a global basis | Prior clearance required as and when this may be considered | Executive decree no. 6/03 of 24 January 2003 (ch. I, art. 1, cl. 3) |
| 22. Application for authorisation to setup and make financial provision for only the local net retention on major claims | As and when required | Executive decree no. 6/03 of 24 January 2003 (ch. II, art. 8) |
| 23. Submission of plans for the process of financial guarantees in respect of reserves constituted by the insurer | Up to 30 April of each year for the previous financial year | Executive decree no. 6/03 of 24 January 2003 (ch. II, art. 13) |
| 24. Submission of a financial recovery plan for insurers with insufficient reserves and/or insufficient financial guarantees | As per the instructions of the regulator following detection of the issue | Executive decree no. 6/03 of 24 January 2003 (ch. II, art. 14) |

| | | |
|---|---|---|
| 25. Presentation of calculation of solvency margin and minimum solvency margin | By 30 April of each year for the immediate previous financial year | Executive decree no. 6/03 of 24 January 2003 (ch. III, art. 24) |
| 26. Financial recovery plan in the event of failure to achieve minimum required solvency margin or insufficient financial guarantees | As per time frames to be fixed by the insurance regulator in each case | Executive decree no. 6/03 of 24 January 2003 (ch. III, art. 23) |
| 27. Submission of completed registration and accounting inspection of guarantees of insurance reserves | Not specified | Decree no. 96/04 of 17 December 2004 (ch. II, art., 6, cl. 4) |
| 28. Submit copies of all necessary documents to the National Directorate of Social Security on WCA insurance rejected by the insurance market but placed with intervention of authorities. | Half-yearly | Decree no. 53/05 of 15 August 2005 (ch. IV, art. 8, cl. 8); required documents to be defined in further regulations |
| 29. Notification to an appropriate court of permanent disability claims of WCA insurance | Within 8 days of discharge | Decree no. 53/05 of 15 August 2005 (ch. V, art. 13, cl. 1) |
| 30. Notification to an appropriate court of WCA insurance temporary disability cases of more than 12 months | Within 8 days after exceeding this time period | Decree no. 53/05 of 15 August 2005 (ch. V, art. 13, cl. 4) |
| 31. Notification of all WCA claims to an appropriate court (reports should be in four copies and contain 18 items in respect of each claim as per sample in annex II to this decree) | Half-yearly | Decree no. 53/05 of 15 August 2005 (ch. V, art. 14) |
| 32. Notification of all WCA occupational illnesses claims to the Provincial Directorate of Health, Social Security provincial directorate, and the employer | Not specified | Decree no. 53/05 of 15 August 2005 (ch. V, art. 15) |
| 33. Notification to an appropriate court of all deaths as a result of WCA insurance accident or occupational illness claims | Notification period for insurers probably 48 hours as per period for health authorities | Decree no. 53/05 of 15 August 2005 (ch. V, art. 16, cl. 3) |
| 34. All insurers to note in their annual accounts their provincial branches in the national territory | Each year with their accounts from 2010 yearend | Executive decree no. 74/07 of 29 June 2007 (art. 3) |
| 35. Statements of performance of business per branch | Periodic reports as per intervals to be defined | Executive decree no. 74/07 of 29 June 2007 (art. 3) |
| 36. Insurers intending to apply their own rating charts for obligatory motor liability should submit them for approval. | As and when required | Decree no. 35/09 of 11 August 2009 (ch. II, art. 13, cl. 2) |
| 37. Notify the regulator of all cases of rejection of motor liability. | As and when this happens | Decree no. 35/09 of 11 August 2009 (ch. II, art. 14, cl. 3) |

| | | |
|---|---|---|
| 38. Annual submission of the motor insurance disc for displaying on windscreen of vehicle | Each year within 15 days of date not specified | Decree no. 35/09 of 11 August 2009 (ch. II, art. 20, cl. 7) |
| 39. Motor liability insurance data for the national data centre | Not defined | Decree no. 35/09 of 11 August 2009 (ch. V, art. 35, cl. 7) |
| 40. Motor quarterly reports of net premium for calculation of 5% levy for the Motor Guarantee Fund (annual adjustment on the basis of annual accounts) | 15 days after the end of each quarter followed by payment within 15 days after issuing of invoice by the fund | Circular no. 01/FGA/MF/10 of 26 April 2010 |
| 41. Accounting balance sheet of the first half-year for each year | 31 July of current year | Circular no. 02/ISS/MF/10 of I July 2010 (ch. II, art. 3) |
| 42. Annual underwriting statistics | 31 January of each year for the immediate previous financial year | Circular no. 02/ISS/MF/10 of I July 2010 (ch. II, art. 4, cl. 1) |
| 43. First half-year underwriting statistics | 31 July of each year for the immediate previous financial year | Circular no. 02/ISS/MF/10 of I July 2010 (ch. II, art. 4, cl. 2) |
| 44. Submission of programme and details of course material for training of insurance agents | 15 days prior to date of commencement of the course | Circular no. 06/ISS/MF/10 of 2 August 2010 (ch. I, art. 1, cl. 2) |
| 45. Nomination of members of evaluation panel | Prior to conducting of the course | Circular no. 06/ISS/MF/10 of 2 August 2010 (ch. I, art. 2, cl. 3) |
| 46. Submission of results of final examination of insurance agents | Not specified | Circular no. 06/ISS/MF/10 of 2 August 2010 (ch. I, art. 2, cl. 6) |
| 47. Application for issuing of certificates for qualifying insurance agents | Not specified | Circular no. 06/ISS/MF/10 of 2 August 2010 (ch. I, art. 3, cl. 3) |
| 48. Quarterly accounts and balance sheet with opinion of auditing committee | Not specified | Presidential decree no. 141/13 of 27 September 2013 (ch. I, art. 4, cl. 3) |
| 49. Report on the establishment of a complaints centre and submission of respective regulations and contact details | Within 10 days after the setting up of the mechanism | Notice no.1/15 of 13 October, 2015 (ch. III, art. 18) |
| 50. Full disclosure to the public of the complaints centre | Not specified | Notice no. 1/15 of 13 October, 2015 (ch. III, art. 20) |
| 51. Report on complaints cases to the regulator | Within 5 days following request by regulator | Notice no.1/15 of 13 October 2015 (ch. II, art. 10, item c., and art. 6, item h.) |

# Appendix V: Intermediary Legal Entities

1. Peritana—Corretagem e Análise de Riscos, Lda
2. Gestiseguro—Corretora e Consultora de Seguros, SA
3. Angorisk—Corretores de Seguros, SA
4. AON—Corretores de Seguros, Lda
5. Pe & Se—Mediação de Seguros, Lda
6. Almeida e Associados—Mediação de Seguros, Lda
7. Nacional Brokers Angola, Lda.
8. GSAA—Corretora de Seguros, SA
9. Interseguros—Corretores de Seguros, SA
10. Deal Seguros—Corretor de Seguros, Lda
11. Imboseguros—Mediação de Seguros, Lda.
12. Corretana—Mediação de Seguros, Lda
13. Porto Seguro—Corretores e Consultores de Resseguros, SA
14. Real Risk—Corretores de Seguros e Resseguros, Lda
15. Work Out Seguros, LDA
16. AIBA—Corretores de Seguros, Lda
17. Inter Broker, LDA
18. RI&A Corretores de Seguros, Lda
19. Moseg Seguros—Corretores de Seguros e Resseguros, SA
20. Cosea Corretora de Seguros em Angola, Lda
21. Crucial Corretora de Seguros, Lda
22. Transeguros Corretora de Seguros, SA
23. Media Seguros, Lda
24. Primum Vivere—Mediação e Corretagem de Seguros, Lda
25. Inter Risk Angola Corretora de Seguros, Lda
26. Alfa Center, Corretora de Seguros, Lda
27. Seguro Único, Lda

28. Risk–Tech—Corretor de Seguros, Lda
29. Avangard Insurance Brokers, Lda
30. Afri—Seguros, Lda
31. Kyeleka Seguros, SA
32. Exu—Mediadores de Seguros Lda.
33. WASEM—Corretora de Seguros e Resseguros, Lda.
34. CP Seguros—Corretores de Seguros, Lda
35. Grand Seguros—Mediação de Seguros, Lda
36. Gerswast—Mediadora de Seguros, Lda
37. Morpheu's—Mediação de Seguros, Lda
38. Estrelaseg—Corretores de Seguros, Lda
39. Ango Insurance—Corretores de Seguros, Lda
40. Assurland Angola Corretores de Seguros, SA
41. Artemwasia—Medidação e Corretagem de Seguros, Lda
42. Liberdade—Mediação de Seguros, Lda
43. Hekandando—Corretora de Seguros Lda
44. VDP—Mediação e Corretagem de Seguros, Lda.
45. Proagil—Corretagem de Seguros, Lda.
46. Eternidade—Mediação de Seguros, Lda
47. EGSA—Corretores de Seguros de Angola SA
48. Sólida—Mediação de Seguros Lda
49. Cormed—Corretagem e Mediação de Seguros, Lda
50. Impelir—Mediação de Seguros
51. Líder AG—Corretora de Seguros Lda
52. N'dapama—Sociedade de Mediação e Seguros
53. Segurbastos
54. Omega
55. Big Seven—Mediação de Seguros, Lda
56. Clarezza—Corretora e Mediadora de Seguros, Lda

Source: List as provided on the website of ARSEG, http://www.arseg.ao/index.php?option=com_content&view=article&id=122&Itemid=161&lang=pt (accessed 30 November 2018)

# Appendix VI: Obligatory Reporting Conditions for Intermediaries

| Reporting Requirements | Reporting Periods | Legislation |
|---|---|---|
| 1. Annual accounts as at 31 December and in accordance with the required chart of accounts | 31 March of each year | Law no. 1/00 of 3 February 2000 and executive decree no. 7/03 of 24 January 2003 (ch. VI, s. III, art. 25, cl. 2, item f) |
| 2. Registration of a tied individual agent that signs an employment contract with an insurer and wants to remain an intermediary | Within 60 days after signing of contract with the insurer | Executive decree no. 7/03 of 24 January 2003 (ch. III, s. I, art. 12) |
| 3. Registration of a tied individual agent that ceases to be an employee of an insurer and wants to remain an intermediary | Within 60 days after cessation of employment contract | Executive Decree no. 7/03 of 24 January 2003 (ch. III, s. II, art. 15) |
| 4. Authorization and registration of an insurance broker | Before commencement of operations | Executive decree no. 7/03 of 24 January 2003 (ch. III, s. III, art. 17) |
| 5. Notify the regulator of any changes to previously submitted information | Within 60 days after verification of the change | Circular no. 06/ISS/MF/10 of 2 August 2010 (ch. III, art. 8, cl. 5) |
| 6. Premium and commissions bordereau | By 30 April of each year | Circular no. 06/ISS/MF/10 of 2 August 2010 (ch. V, art. 13, cl. 2, item a) |
| 7. Claims bordereau | By 30 April of each year | Circular no. 06/ISS/MF/10 of 2 August 2010 (ch. V, art. 13, cl. 2, item b) |
| 8. Tax payments report | By 30 April of each year | Circular no. 06/ISS/MF/10 of 2 August 2010 (ch. V, art. 13, cl. 2, item c) |
| 9. Social Security payments report | By 30 April of each year | Circular no. 06/ISS/MF/10 of 2 August 2010 (ch. V, art. 13, cl. 2, item d) |

# Index

CPSIA information can be obtained
at www.ICGtesting.com
Printed in the USA
BVHW031050190419
546009BV00005B/11/P